BUGS VS HUMANS

BUGS VS HUMANS

by Peter Heule
with illustrations by
Peter Tyler

BLUE
BIKE
BOOKS

The Publisher: Blue Bike Books

Website: www.bluebikebooks.com

Library and Archives Canada Cataloguing in Publication

Heule, Peter, 1980–

Bugs vs. humans / Peter Heule.

ISBN 978-1-897278-37-6

1. Medical parasitology—Miscellanea. I. Title.

QL496.12.H48 2009   616.9'6002   C2009-900185-3

Project Director: Nicholle Carrière
Project Editor: Pat Price
Cover Image: Images courtesy of ©Dallas photography | Dreamstime.com; ©Isselee | Dreamstime.com; Photos.com
Back Cover Image: Photos.com
Illustrations: Peter Tyler
Photos: dreamstime.com: pages 23, 28, 36, 45, 50, 77, 93, 107, 146, 154, 158, 175, 177, 193, 223; photos.com: pages 41, 72, 117, 122, 127, 150, 166, 169, 190, 211, 215, 228, 231

We acknowledge the support of the Alberta Foundation for the Arts for our publishing program.

We acknowledge the financial support of the Government of Canada through the Book Publishing Industry Development Program (BPIDP) for our publishing activities.

Canadian   Patrimoine
Heritage   canadien

PC: P1

Dedication

Thanks to my parents Nancy and Mark for their encouragement (and lack of discouragement) of my interest in every creature I ever brought home.

For my lovely wife Robyn, without your patience and support this would not have been possible. Who else would catch my spiders off the ceiling on their lunch break?

Acknowledgments

I would like to thank my wife, Robyn, for her patience with this project. Also my colleagues Tyler Cobb, Matthias Buck, David Walter and Rob Hinchliffe from the Royal Alberta Museum's Invertebrate Zoology department for their suggestions and advice. Lastly, I would like to thank all the animals of the world for their contributions to the Earth's ecosystems and for continuing inspiration.

Contents

Bugs vs Humans

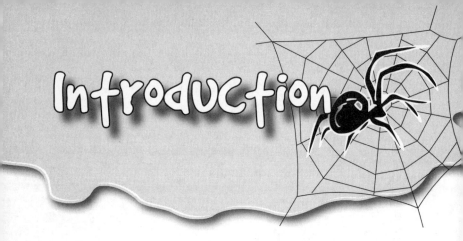

Introduction

Why do humans dislike bugs so much? Is it because they sting and bite? Because they chew on our flowers and destroy trees and crops? Or maybe it's because some of them are downright creepy, icky and even gross. Shouldn't mosquitoes and cockroaches all be wiped out? After all, what good are they?

Believe it or not, bugs are not our enemies. In fact, even the smallest creatures are important to the web of life. Insects have been around for hundreds of millions of years—they were here long before humans were. More than a million different species of insects are still around, playing a huge variety of roles—as decomposers, pollinators, farmers, bloodsuckers—to keep the Earth's ecosystems functioning.

We can learn a lot from insects. As some of the oldest land animals, insects have experienced problems that all organisms (including humans) face—finding food, finding mates, trying not to be eaten, avoiding parasites—and, over the millennia, they have found solutions as varied as they are. We can learn from their experience! And, although humans might be the dominant life form on Earth, we didn't always occupy this position. Way back in prehistoric times, our ancestors were often eaten by bigger, stronger animals. Luckily, our ancestors figured out how to create weapons, and, working together, they hunted and devoured their way to the top of the food chain. It wasn't all woolly mammoth sandwiches, though. When times were tough and game was scarce, insects could be relied on for food.

Bugs are still a source of food for many humans around the world. But they are also sources of medicines, pest control, dye, silk and even inspiration! If the world didn't have pollinating insects, such as bees and flies, to fertilize flowers, we'd have no fruits, nuts or vegetables to eat. Cattle are raised on grasses and grains that flourish because tiny soil insects and mites keep soil fertile, and even fish dine on insects. So, even if you don't eat insects, you certainly benefit from the fruits of their labour.

I believe that most people dislike insects and spiders, not because they were bitten or stung in childhood but because they were grossed out by killing an insect. I still remember squishing a Western tent caterpillar with a bike lock when I was in first grade. Guts went every-where; there was a hideous mess, and it was all by my hand. Think about it. What if your first experience with a goldfish involved you stomping on one? Think about the mess it would create and how gross it would be. Would you maybe dislike goldfish when you got older? I'll bet bug haters have some hidden memory of the time they squashed a bug as a kid, and that's the real reason they're disgusted by insects.

It's unacceptable—even illegal—to kill or hurt small ani-mals, such as kittens or puppies. Yet, people kill insects all the time, without a second thought. If it makes no difference to you whether some small creature lives or dies, why choose death? The next time you see an insect, choose to let it live. Insects are worth far more to us alive than they are stuck to the bottom of your shoe.

Insect Origins

Arthropod Evolution

It is believed that life on Earth began some 3.8 billion years ago and that all the living organisms we see today—bacteria, protists (mostly single-celled organisms), plants, animals and fungus—descended from a common ancestor, probably a single-celled bacterium. Why do we think this? Because all living creatures use DNA as blueprints to repair and replace the cells of their bodies. This DNA is like a set of instructions for life; whether you're a fungus, a plant or a human, the instructions for growth, reproduction and survival are all written in the same language. Animals (and that includes humans), for example, all share similar chunks of DNA called HOX genes. These genes help shape the body and the head and are responsible for all those great things such as eyes, mouths and brains. All life on Earth uses DNA, which means that if you look far enough into the past, we are all related. We are all family.

Branching Out

Over the millions of years since it first originated, life diversified. Some single-celled organisms evolved into multicelled life forms, and then these multicelled creatures further evolved in response to their environments. As their body shapes and sizes began to change in different ways, they branched off into groups with similar characteristics. For example, some organisms became plants and used light to obtain their food; others became fungi and bacteria, which absorbed food from their surroundings; and some became animals, which ingested their food. Some organisms remained simple and small, others became large and more complex, developing body structures to help them sense the world around them, to move, to eat and to protect themselves.

The similarities between organisms allow scientists to place living things in categories. For example, all animals with backbones, such as fish, amphibians, reptiles, birds and mammals, are vertebrates. They share the characteristic of having a spinal column, something they all inherited from a common ancestor.

Who's Who:
the Animal Family Tree

The categories in which scientists place all living things are divided up into smaller categories, which are divided into even smaller categories. This is called "classification." The largest categories are called kingdoms, and all life is divided into five of them: bacteria, protists, fungi, plants and animals. Each kingdom is then divided into phyla (phylum is the singular term). Humans belong to the animal kingdom, of course, in phylum Chordata, which includes animals with backbones. Along with us in this category are other animals with backbones, such as fish, amphibians, reptiles, birds and other mammals. Other phyla include the unsegmented yet worm-like Nematoda, such as round worms and thread worms, possibly the most abundant organisms on Earth; Mollusca, snails, clams, squid and octopus, with almost 100,000 species worldwide; Annelida, the worms; and

Arthropoda, which includes insects, centipedes, spiders and crustaceans, such as lobsters and shrimp.

These phyla are further divided into classes. For example, a subgroup of phylum Chordata is class Mammalia, the mammals. Classes are divided into orders, orders are divided into families, families into genera (singular: genus) and genera into species. What does the human family tree look like? Kingdom Animalia, phylum Chordata, class Mammalia, order Primates, family Hominidae (the great apes: man, chimpanzees, gorillas and orangutans), genus *Homo* and species *sapiens*.

Whew!

Bug Bite

Did you know that most of our favourite animals are chordates? Yet they make up less than 3 percent of the animal kingdom.

Introducing...Arthropods

Insects belong to the phylum Arthropoda. Arthropods are animals with segmented bodies and many pairs of jointed limbs. Unlike humans, they don't have an internal skeleton or a backbone. Instead, they have a hard, external skeleton called an exoskeleton. Arthropods are the largest phylum in the animal kingdom, with the insects, arachnids, centipedes, millipedes and various kinds of crustaceans included in their own classes. For example, a Seven-spotted ladybug's family tree would look like this: Kingdom Animalia, phylum Arthropoda, class Insecta, order Coleoptera, family Coccinellidae, genus *Coccinella* and species *septempunctata*.

Although lobsters and crabs are arthropods, they, along with mantis shrimp and krill, are part of the class Malacostraca, distant cousins of the insects. More than 80 percent of the world's animal species are arthropods and, of them, 95 percent are insects. That means if we count the million or so insects that have been discovered, they make up almost two thirds of all species of life!

Arthropods are also the most diverse phylum—more than a million species are known to science. This number is pretty impressive, when you consider that the number of species of *all living things known to science* is about 1.7 million. To compare, there are only 5416 species of mammals, and 236 of them are primates, such as monkeys, lemurs, apes and humans. And, when it comes to family size, insects rule. For example, there are about 37 species in the cat family, compared to 16,500 species of scarab beetles and 60,000 species of *Ichneumonid* wasps. Even the largest family of mammals, the rats and mice (family Muridae), has only 650 species worldwide.

Bug Bite

The insect population at any given time is estimated to be 10 quintillion (a quintillion is 1 followed by 19 zeros). That means they outnumber us humans 1,492,000,000 to one.

The First Animals

Although *life* had already been lurking in our primordial oceans for some time, the first *animals* didn't appear until roughly 600 million years ago. Unlike the other Earthlings of the day—protists and bacteria, which used light or absorbed their food—these organisms, for the very first time, could ingest food. They could make a meal out of entire organisms, instead of just soaking up small particles. The development of a mouth was a defining moment in animal history, and much of animal evolution since then has involved finding new things to eat. Ingesting more food provided these organisms with more energy and ultimately allowed them to grow larger. In time, they evolved to become more complex than the other single-celled organisms they shared the planet with. Over time, they gained structures such as cilia and flagella, which acted like oars to help them swim. They also developed new and clever ways to find and capture prey, eventually becoming multicellular organisms, with different cells devoted to carrying out different functions in the body.

Bug Bite

Our primate ancestors weren't scratching out a living with their fingernails (an heirloom to be sure) until after the end of the dinosaur age, about 60 million years ago. The human family Hominidae didn't show up for another 35 million years or so, and our genus *Homo* is a mere 2 to 2.5 million years old. So, technically, the insects should be considered our elders and treated with the respect they deserve.

The Cambrian Explosion

By 544 million years ago, the oceans were home to primitive chordates, arthropod crustaceans and annelid worms, all with different overall body shapes. The chordates hadn't yet developed into anything we would recognize and looked more like worms or eels without backbones. Worms, just as they do today, had legless, segmented bodies that served their burrowing lifestyle perfectly, and the arthropods were already looking rather shrimp-like.

How do we know what they looked like? Because of fossils. This was the Cambrian period, when life flourished and diversified in the oceans. Animals were forming shells and skeletons that preserved better than soft body parts, and, for the first time, they left fossils behind. Even then, almost all of the major animal groups were present, and, during this period, new and wonderful varieties of creatures came to be. Fossils from this period are the first evidence we have of the existence of arthropods.

Trilobites

Approximately 500 million years ago, in the Cambrian period, there were more varieties of animals than the world had ever seen, or has seen since. All this life was still swimming about in the oceans, with dry land not yet colonized by much more than the odd patch of algae. The most abundant and obvious creatures of the day were arthropods. They ranged from very small to very large and occupied the role of top predator for millions of years. Some of the most numerous arthropods in the seas were trilobites. Probably the most-recognized fossils, trilobites looked a little like well-armoured cockroaches, though they were more crustacean-like. They had one pair of antennae and compound eyes, characteristics that insects would eventually come to possess. It is said that trilobites ruled the seas, though they probably spent most of their time on the bottom searching for dead matter to eat. They existed for millions of years, eventually disappearing, as the Earth's climate and ecosystems changed.

Bug Bite

One of the best places to see 500-million-year-old animal fossils is the Burgess Shale in Yoho National Park. The ancient animals left behind mineralized impressions of their bodies, and some forms have never been seen since then. Not only are they weird and amazing, compared to modern animals, but they also were some of the first to have shells and other hard body parts that could become fossils for us to see today. If you want to peer into the distant past at animals that have long since disappeared, Burgess Shale is the place to do it.

Water Scorpions

In this age of arthropods, giant swimming *Eurypterids* called water scorpions, distant relatives of today's horseshoe crabs and arachnids, enjoyed a position at the top of the food chain. They looked more like the scorpions we see today than any other recognizable animal, and some, such as *Jaekelopterus rhenania*, reached lengths of 2 metres! It's no surprise that smaller arthropods and other animals began to develop better eyesight around this time—they needed to keep watch for hungry water scorpions swimming above.

Land Ho!

As dry land emerged from the oceans, so did the arthropods, possibly seeking refuge from hungry water scorpions or just a new place to eat. Some of the oldest evidence of life on land are ichnofossils from almost 450 million years ago. These fossils are believed to be burrows and tracks from enormous millipedes, cousins of the insects, a metre long and as thick as your leg! As land came to be colonized by primitive plants, many arthropod groups came, too. First came the decomposers, feeding on dead plant matter. They were followed by the predators that fed on the decomposers. Later, herbivores, which ate living plants, moved in to take advantage of the lush landscape.

Finally—Insects!

With land came the land-loving arthropods we know so well. Some of the most primitive insects were also the earliest to leave us signs of their existence. Springtails (*Collembola*), tiny insect relatives with internal mouthparts, were providing fossil evidence almost 400 million years ago. Bristletails (*Archaeognatha*), wingless primitive insects, appear in the fossil record about 370 million years ago, followed closely by the spiders (*Araneae*) that have made a living off the insects on land for at least 360 million years. There are even fossil cockroaches (*Blattodea*), mayflies (*Ephemeroptera*) and weird cricket-grasshoppers (*Orthoptera*) more than 300 million years old that bear remarkable similarities to modern families.

Bug Bite

Springtails got their name from their ability to catapult themselves into the air using a tail-like structure (called a *furcula*) on the underside of their body. Today, springtails are some of the world's most abundant soil organisms; each square metre of dirt can contain upwards of 100,000 of them! They are vital decomposers that help recycle nutrients from the dead matter within the soil.

Here Were Giants

The Carboniferous (359–299 BC) and early Permian (299–circa 251 BC) periods swarmed with arthropods. In fact, more varieties were around at that time than there are now. There were plenty of small insects, spiders, millipedes (*Diplopoda*) and centipedes (Chilopoda), just as there are today. There were also giants: water scorpions more than 2 metres long, giant centipedes measuring 1.5 metres—even the true scorpions (Scorpiones), such as *Brontoscopio anglicus*, were a metre long, with light-bulb-sized stingers. Primitive dragonfly relatives called Griffinflies (*Meganisoptera*) cruised through the swampy air; some, such as *Meganeuropsis permiana*, with their 74-centimetre wingspans, were the largest insects ever.

Some extinct insect groups were already equipped to pierce and suck plant juices—and they must have done a lot of it to reach body lengths of 70 centimetres. These insects' larger body size probably kept them off the menu for the emerging amphibians (Amphibia), our closest relatives at the time, which were stretching their new walking legs by 365 million years ago.

Take a Deep Breath

There were some seriously large bugs around in the Carboniferous period. Why were they so big? The land in those days was lush with plant life that produced huge quantities of oxygen. In fact, it's thought that the atmosphere then contained as much as 32 percent oxygen, compared to the 21 percent we have today. The extra oxygen made it possible for big bugs to exist for two reasons. First, big bugs need more oxygen than small bugs, though both breathe through the same simple system of tubes. The higher concentration of oxygen made it possible for big bugs to get enough air without having to gasp for more. Second, because oxygen allows animals to burn energy and keep their cells working, more oxygen means faster growth and larger body size.

The climate at the time was also humid and warm, fine conditions for "cold-blooded" (ectothermic) animals. There was plenty of food, in the form of plants, and the high temperatures allowed the animals to grow faster—

an insect that always has plenty of food and lives in an area that's as warm as bathwater can grow much larger than an insect that goes hungry in the cold. This is why we see so many large insects, spiders and reptiles in the lush, tropical regions of the world.

Bug Bite

"Cold-blooded" (ectothermic) doesn't mean an animal has cold blood. It really means that an animal's internal temperature is the same as the outside. So, if it is 30°C outside, an ectothermic animal's inside temperature is also 30°C.

All Great Bugs Must Come to an End

The tropical climate of the Carboniferous period gave insects and other land arthropods a head start over the vertebrates as landlubbers. But the glory days of high oxygen and gigantism didn't last forever. In fact, the name "Carboniferous" hints at what happened during that period. All that extra oxygen, the high temperatures and lush forests led to some pretty serious forest fires, leaving behind the charred coal beds that humans now mine for fossil fuels. Thanks in part to these fires, oxygen levels slowly fell, and carbon dioxide levels rose. The giant arthropods disappeared over the Permian period, not forever, but until the oxygen levels rose again near the end of the dinosaur age in the Cretaceous period.

Bug Bite

Arthropods had a 100-million-year head start on the dinosaurs. By the time anything even resembling an amphibian first crawled onto dry land, the arthropods had already made themselves at home. They even weathered some of the first ice ages, about 440 million years ago.

Taking to the Air

Although it might be every kid's dream to fly like a bird, our feathered friends were hardly pioneers in the field. Before the first birds tasted the air, about 220 million years ago, reptiles known as Pterosaurs flapped around on leathery wings. The largest animal to ever fly was a member of this group; called Quetzalcoatlus, it had a wingspan of 12 metres, the size of a small plane! However, insects were flying before Pterosaurs. The first animals ever to fly, insects have had a long time to get the hang of it. They are still the best flyers around, and some flies are capable of manoeuvres that no bird, bat or aircraft can rival.

Bug Bite

Two-winged flies, such as Houseflies (Muscidae: *Musca domestica*), are hard to swat because they can detect the tiniest movements and respond too quickly for us to get at them. As they buzz about, they make hundreds of corrections per second, thanks in part to their tiny hind wings, called *halteres*. They act like little gyroscopes, telling the fly which direction is up and which way they are moving.

Getting Your Wings

Exactly when insects conquered flight is unknown. However, fossil evidence suggests that it might have been almost 400 million years ago. No one really knows how insects managed to develop wings without first converting a pair of limbs, either, though there are some ideas. One is that insects that had external gills emerging from their abdomen and thorax as aquatic nymphs (young insects that resemble adults) found another, aerodynamic use for them as adults on dry land. Other theories suggest that wings developed from non-moving lobes on the thorax or from small branches of the leg segments nearest the body.

Proto-types

Insects probably didn't start flying the moment their proto-wings emerged. At first, these wing-like structures likely helped to heat or cool the body, much like the sail on the back of reptiles such as *Dimetrodon*. Proto-wings might also have served insects as camouflage, as protection for their legs or as a way to reduce water loss, by covering up their spiracles (tiny holes through which insects, centipedes and millipedes breathe).

Falling with Style

So, how did insects develop the ability to fly? We can get a good idea of the answer by looking at the behaviour of modern-day insects that live high in the tree canopies of tropical rainforests. Gliding—or falling with grace and some control—is common among canopy animals. Tree-dwelling tarantulas, frogs, snakes, lizards, squirrels, marsupials and colugos (a.k.a. flying lemurs, though they aren't lemurs)—none of which have wings—have all developed the ability to either parachute or glide.

Even bristletails, a primitive insect group that predates wings, have been shown to glide back to the tree trunk from which they fell, with ease and accuracy. These bristletails give us a picture of how gliding behaviour could help an early insect survive, even without working wings. If trees and food are widely spaced, then gliding could be an effective method of moving from one tree to the next without ever risking a trip to the ground. As the living gliders show us, leaping from a branch into the air could also be a good way to get a predator off your tail.

Worker ants of several species can glide, too—although they're wingless, they can use the movements of their bodies and limbs to control their descent.

Learning to Fly

By 300 million years ago, proto-wings were becoming more and more sophisticated, and insects were leaving behind fossil impressions of a variety of lovely veined wings. Presumably, as they got better at gliding and developed the muscles involved in flight, insects gained the ability to fly without having to fall off something first. It is not known exactly how the modern wings evolved from proto-wings, but if the fossil evidence is correct, then insects beat those flying Pterosaurs in the race for flight by almost 100 million years! Mammals didn't catch up until the bats (Chiroptera) took wing 55 to 65 million years ago. To be fair, true mammals didn't arise until the middle of the dinosaur age, about 200 million years ago, so maybe the bats can't be faulted for arriving late.

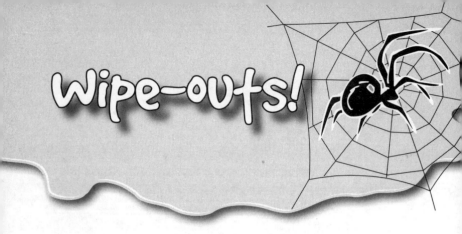

Wipe-outs!

Earth has experienced five mass extinctions that we know about: the Ordovician-Silurian, about 450 million years ago; the Late Devonian, about 364 million years ago; the Permian-Triassic, about 250 million years ago; the End Triassic, about 199 to 214 million years ago; and the Cretaceous-Tertiary, about 65 million years ago.

The Permian-Triassic Extinction

The greatest loss ever suffered by life on Earth was the Permian-Triassic, or End Permian, extinction, which wiped out more than 90 percent of all species in the oceans and 70 percent of land-dwelling reptiles, amphibians, insects and plants. Nine insect orders became extinct, and another 10 were seriously affected. That's 19 of the 22 orders that were around back then.

No one knows exactly what caused this mass die-out, but it was thought to be the result of a combination of factors. At the time, the carbon dioxide levels in the air were higher than they are today, the climate was dry, continents were drifting such that ocean currents changed, entire chains of volcanoes were blasting mineral dust into the atmosphere and there might also have been some meteor impacts, just to make it interesting.

The Cretaceous-Tertiary Extinction

The most well-known mass extinction must be the Cretaceous-Tertiary Extinction, better known as the K-T event that snuffed out the dinosaurs. About 70 percent of the world's living things disappeared in this event, which is thought to have been caused by a huge asteroid impact. But the extinction wasn't entirely the fault of the asteroid. Leading up to the impact, widespread climate change led to changes in the plants that dinosaurs relied on for food. This put the dinosaurs in a tough position—they needed lots of food to support their huge size, but there was less available. Once the asteroid hit, it sent so much dust into the atmosphere that the skies darkened, leading to a very long impact winter. Although this event finished off the dinosaurs, the number of animal species that became extinct didn't compare to the Permian extinction—and it barely made a dent in the insect population, according to the fossil record. No doubt many billions of insects died, and some families disappeared altogether, but, unlike the dinosaurs, they survived.

Bug Bite

Insects can teach us many things, should we choose to pay heed. They have survived at least four out of five mass-extinction events in Earth's history. Maybe we should look to the insects for solutions to human problems, such as how to survive climate change, meteor impacts and other catastrophes.

The Survivors

Other than the fleas, all the major insect orders we see today were around to watch the final act of the reptile age. Arthropod plant feeders were likely the hardest hit, thanks to the trillions of tons of debris that the asteroid sent into the atmosphere. All that dust led to months of darkness, known as impact winter, which prevented plants and algae from growing and eventually made temperatures drop. This in turn starved the herbivores, making life difficult for the predators. Chances are, the best strategy in such times would have been to scavenge, and 4300 or more species of cockroaches can't be wrong. Being small, feeding on dead plant and animal matter and being able to wait out or avoid nasty conditions helped the insects weather the storm and survive to this day.

Bugs, Inside and Out

Using one's Head

Insects are incredibly varied in their shape, size and life-style. Yet, despite their differences, all insects have three major body parts: the head, thorax and abdomen. The head holds the eyes, mouth, brain and antennae—it's the body's communication and control centre. The thorax is the workforce: the wings (when present), six legs and the muscles that move them are housed here. The abdomen is where the guts and reproductive organs are found and where fat is stored; it's essentially the power plant and storage warehouse of the insect body.

Bug Bite

Although insects do have brains, they are not as sophisticated as ours. When it comes to processing information from the eyes, mouthparts and other senses, they function in a similar way to our brains. Perhaps most importantly, the insect brain is the source of hormones (chemical messengers) that control growth, moulting and behaviour.

Bugs, Inside and Out

Getting a Head

Although insects might seem about as close to alien life-forms as you could find on Earth, they aren't entirely different from us. All animals share HOX genes, which are responsible for determining body shape and head structure. The HOX genes you carry help shape *your* head, torso and abdomen, and the ones insects carry shape *their* head, thorax and abdomen. This is true of all animals that still bother to develop a head. Like yours, an insect head contains eyes that see movement and colour, mouthparts that can taste and devour food and a brain to make sense of it all.

Bug Bite

Some animals do not have a head. Adult sea stars, sand dollars and urchins and their relatives have no head region.

Getting a Feel for Things

Insects don't have noses, because they smell using their antennae. As an insect waves its antennae around, tiny particles floating in the air or water touch the sensitive surfaces, and a signal is sent to the insect's brain. The same thing happens when we smell something in the air—our smell receptors send a signal to our brain, which recognizes the smell as, for example, barbecue smoke or a nearby skunk.

Antennae are also referred to as "feelers"—and feel they do; in fact, insect feelers have a keen sense of touch. But they can also taste and smell and can even detect heat and moisture. Having two finely tuned smeller-taster-feeler-heat-and-moisture-seekers mounted to their heads allows insects, centipedes and millipedes to smell, taste and feel their way through life. The type of smells or tastes an insect's antennae are sensitive to depends on what it uses them for.

Home Smelly Home

Female mosquitoes (Diptera: Culicidae) ready to lay their eggs use their senses of smell and taste to look for a suitable puddle or pond. They use smell to zero in on a good site, and then they taste the water surface with their feet and mouth-parts. Tasting tells them if the right kinds of food organisms are present and if there are mosquito-killing bacteria around. Because the mother will never be around to see her eggs hatch, the best she can do as a parent is choose a safe place in which to leave them.

Bug Bite

Like you, insects taste using their mouthparts. Some insects, such as butterflies (Lepidoptera) and hoverflies (Diptera: Syrphidae), can also taste with their feet. This allows them to sample a flower's nectar as they land. Can you imagine tasting with the bottoms of your feet? I bet you'd change your socks more often.

Don't Make Me Use These!

The most impressive antennae of all are found in the
long-horned beetle family (Cerambycidae), some of which
have antennae longer than their body. Their oversized
antennae help them locate trees that are unhealthy, dead
or dying in which to lay their eggs. They can smell chemicals the trees give off when injured, pheromones used to
gather enough beetles to overcome the trees' defenses,
and can detect the opposite sex. In some species, male
long-horned beetles actually fight with their antennae,
like gladiators, bashing and tripping each other until
someone's had enough and leaves. The victor is then free
to court the nearby females, without competition—until
another male shows up.

Open Wide

Insect mouthparts are specifically shaped to deal with the kind of food insects eat. Many insects have biting and chewing mouthparts, which work well for chomping up vegetable and animal matter. Some wood-boring beetles (families Cerambycidae and Buprestidae) can even chew through soft metals such as aluminum and copper, thanks to jaws built to chew into tree bark. The mouthparts of insects with liquid diets are specialized to work with liquid food: the straw-like beaks that aphids and other bugs (members of the order Hemiptera), for example, use to suck plant juices, and the stabbing, cutting, blood-sucking mouths of mosquitoes.

Bug Bite

Some adult insects, such as silk moths and crane flies, don't have functioning digestive systems, because they don't eat after becoming adults. Some can still poop on you, though, with saved-up goop called meconium, which is left over from metamorphosis.

The Butterflies' Dirty Little Secret

Butterflies and moths have special coiled mouthparts, called proboscides (singular: proboscis), which they use like a straw to suck up nectar from flowers. Moths and butterflies, males especially, also use their proboscides to obtain salts and other hard-to-find nutrients from rotting fruit, carrion, mud, puddles of urine and even feces. It's not uncommon to find several butterflies clustered on fresh coyote or other carnivore poop, with their mouthparts probing for substances they don't get from their otherwise nectar-heavy diet. They can actually become drunk if they ingest too much.

If you want to attract butterflies to see this behaviour, called puddling, you (with your parents' help) can make your own mixture of rotting fruit, beer or cider, sugar or molasses and even a splash of urine, and then let it ferment for a couple days. If you choose the right time of year and location to try this experiment—say, late summer in a blooming meadow—you might draw a startling number of butterflies and moths.

Bug Bite

Insects can detect light through their exoskeleton, though more as a seasonal calendar than a watch. They can tell when the days are getting longer or shorter but cannot tell the exact time of day.

Seeing the Light

Just like other animals, insects use their eyes to see the world. As larvae, insects that pupate or undergo complete metamorphosis, such as butterflies and beetles, have simple eyes called stemmata that only detect light intensity, not fine detail. Adult insects and some nymphs (juvenile insects that don't pupate) have special small eyes called ocelli, usually found on the top of the head arranged in a triangle. Like the stemmata, they are used more for detecting small changes in the amount of light present than for formation of images. Ocelli tell an insect what time of day it is and where the horizon is during its airborne acrobatics.

Look into My Compound Eyes

Compound eyes tell an insect what's going on around it. Each compound eye can contain as many as 30,000 lenses—unlike the human eye, which has only one lens per eyeball. Because the lenses in a compound eye are so small, they don't pick up the sort of detail that our eyes do, but they are quite sensitive to movement. Imagine a wall of televisions, like you would see at a home stereo store, all showing the same commercial. If you were to stand back, so that all you could see were the televisions, and the screen image moved, you would see that movement on every television at the same time. This is somewhat like an insect's vision, a kaleidoscope of about the same thing. To a dragonfly with 60,000 lenses to see through, a buzzing fly would seem like a swarm. The compound eyes ensure that no small movements are missed, so the dragonfly can track the motion of the fly, even as the fly performs evasive maneuvers.

Seeing in the Dark

An insect's compound eyes can convert from day vision to night vision. In our eyes, a single lens focuses light onto light-sensitive areas (rods and cones on the retina), which send messages to the brain. In an insect's eye, each lens is the outer layer of an individual ommatidium, which is like a simple elongated version of an eye, with receptors at the base. These ommatidia are the units that make up the compound eye. For daytime vision, each ommatidium only processes light from its own lens. For dawn and dusk light levels, ommatidia can process light from any nearby lens, including their own. To see in the dark, any ommatidium in the insect eye can receive light from any lens in that eye. This allows light from any lens in the compound eye to hit any receptor, so the insects can see in almost total darkness.

Wearing Your Skeleton on the outside

The most obvious difference between insects and humans is our skin. Our skin is soft and flexible. The "skin" of most insects is hard, except in certain places such as the neck and knees. That's because insects wear their skeletons on the outside. This external skeleton, or exoskeleton, and jointed limbs are features shared by all arthropods, including crabs, shrimp, millipedes, centipedes, spiders and scorpions. The exoskeleton defines the outside of an arthropod, and it varies from species to species; the different colours of butterflies and beetles and the variety of shapes and textures of insects, arachnids and crustaceans are the result of variations in the exoskeleton.

Form Follows Function

Thanks to the shape and structure of the exoskeleton that covers them, insect legs can vary from one insect to another, depending on what they're used for. Stick insects have simple walking legs; grasshoppers and crickets have thick, jumping hind legs; diving beetles sport hairy oars; and mantids use their spiny, curved forelegs to catch and then secure their prey while they eat it.

Armoured Bugs

The exoskeleton is like a suit of armour, protecting an insect's soft insides. It's made of a tough compound called chitin, which is glazed with a harder substance called sclerotin. Varying chitin thickness and degrees of sclerotization (the process that hardens and waterproofs the exoskeleton) can mean the difference between the thin, flexible skin of a caterpillar and the tough, thick coating of an adult beetle. Even a thickly armoured beetle has a few soft spots, however, such as the knees and neck, where the skin is thin enough to allow them to move. Predators can use these weak points to gain access to even the most well-armoured insects. For example, a mantid goes straight for the neck when it grabs hold of a bee or beetle.

Bug Bite

Most people think of bugs (that is, land-dwelling arthropods) as squishy, probably because when you step on one, it squishes. This is more a matter of how many thousand times heavier you are than an insect or spider than it is about squishiness. If an animal more than a thousand times your weight—a blue whale, say—were to step on you, you would squish just as easily. In fact, insect exoskeleton is just as dense and strong as human bone.

Under Pressure

An insect's head and thorax are protected by well-armoured, thick layers of exoskeleton, with pillars to provide internal support during chewing and flight. The pillars and the thick exoskeleton prevent the head and thorax from bending or deforming under pressure, when the jaw and flight muscles pull against them. The human jaw works in a similar way: if your jaw muscles were stronger than your bones, you could break your jaw just by chewing too hard! Muscles must be attached to something solid enough to withstand the forces they create when they flex.

Insect Wetsuits

A bug's exoskeleton not only protects it from damage, it also keeps it from drying out, which is a constant threat for land animals. Centipedes, which lack a waxy waterproof layer in their exoskeleton, need a humid environment; without it, they can die of dehydration (ever seen a shrivelled centipede in the corner of a basement?). If crustaceans out of the water don't keep their gills wet, they suffocate. That's why we don't see many crustaceans outside of watery environments—hermit crabs tend to stick close to the seashore, and sow bugs always congregate under logs and stones. Arachnids, millipedes and insects have exoskeletons that are relatively waterproof, like a wetsuit for living on land. This waterproof armour has allowed them to survive on land for hundreds of millions of years.

Moulting, Mending and Metamorphosis

All arthropods, including insects, moult or shed their old exoskeletons. Like snakes shedding their skin, they do this so they can grow. Once an insect moults, it grows quickly in size, before the newly exposed exoskeleton that was underneath hardens. Insects that do not undergo metamorphosis, such as mantids and grasshoppers, moult not just for growth but also for repair. The exoskeleton, which is subject to wear and tear, doesn't repair itself constantly, like our skin does. Instead, arthropods replace all their skin all at once, which makes moulting quite a process.

Growth Spurts

Insects don't grow in the same way that humans do. Until we're adults and stop growing, we grow a little bit every day, so we don't really notice it happening—until we realize we need new shoes because our feet don't fit into the old ones anymore. Insects have to limit their growth spurts to the few minutes between the time they peel themselves out of the old skin and when the new one dries and hardens. The insect can only expand and grow to the next size while the new exoskeleton is still soft.

Guess My Age

Most insects moult a certain number of times over their lifespan, which makes it easy to tell what stage an insect is in but doesn't necessarily tell their age. The growth that occurs between the time they shed the old skin and the new skin hardens depends on how well fed the insects are. An insect that's fed less takes longer to get around to moulting than a well-fed insect does and might not grow as much. Because an underfed insect has the option of delaying a moult or only having a small growth spurt, it's hard to tell how old it is just by looking at it. In species that are much larger than their close relatives, the added size often results from extra moults and growth spurts over the course of the insect's life. By moulting more often than their smaller relatives, larger species can reach a greater adult size without having to make huge size changes with every shed.

Pulling Your Leg

Except for the primitive bristletails (Archaeognatha) and silverfish (Thysanura), insects quit moulting once they reach adulthood. This means that most adult insects cannot grow larger or replace their exoskeleton to repair damage. All of that must occur before they reach adulthood. If a young insect loses a leg, it usually takes two moults to grow it back, one to rebuild a tiny working version of the original and another to grow it to the proper size. Some groups, such as the stick insects (Phasmatodea), will actually let a leg come off, if one is grabbed by a predator. This is called limb autotomy. If a predator seizes the insect by a limb, the insect can intentionally disconnect the leg by means of special muscles and make an escape. The predator is left with a twitching limb, but the insect survives to see another day. If the limb-challenged insect has two moults left before reaching adulthood, it should look normal as an adult. If not, well, the benefit of having six legs is that you can get by with fewer.

My, How You've Changed!

Some insects, such as bees (Hymenoptera), beetles (Coleoptera), butterflies (Lepidoptera) and flies (Diptera) undergo what is called complete metamorphosis. Insects that undergo metamorphosis look completely different as juveniles than they do as adults, unlike insects such as grasshoppers and cockroaches, which look the same throughout their lives, except for getting larger and maybe growing wings. Complete metamorphosis allows an insect to live one lifestyle as a larva, with the appropriate body form and adaptations, and another entirely different lifestyle as an adult.

It is believed that metamorphosis ensures that parents and their offspring are not competing for the same resources (although some groups do feed on the same thing in the same place, regardless of life stage). A caterpillar, for example, is built to eat, expand and grow quickly while food is plentiful. Then it transforms within a cocoon or chrysalis into an adult moth or butterfly that's built to flap around drinking nectar, pollinating and looking for a mate. It's like building two different animals from the same original egg.

Extreme Makeover, Insect-style

Although it might seem that the transformation from larva to adult is simply a matter of adding wings and maybe some longer legs, in reality, metamorphosis is more complicated than that. The larva's body is almost completely torn down and rebuilt, and only a very few original structures, such as the brain, remain. The stage that actually transforms from larva to adult is called the pupa (plural: pupae), and insects are said to pupate or go through pupation.

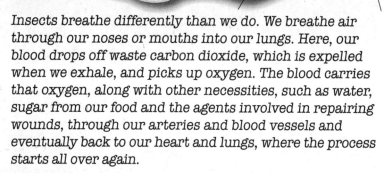

The Inside Scoop

Insects breathe differently than we do. We breathe air through our noses or mouths into our lungs. Here, our blood drops off waste carbon dioxide, which is expelled when we exhale, and picks up oxygen. The blood carries that oxygen, along with other necessities, such as water, sugar from our food and the agents involved in repairing wounds, through our arteries and blood vessels and eventually back to our heart and lungs, where the process starts all over again.

Insects breathe through tiny holes in the abdomen called spiracles. The spiracles lead to tiny hollow tubes called trachea that branch out and run through the entire body. Air passes through this ventilation system in much the same way as heating ducts distribute heat and air in human buildings.

Only in the Movies

Part of the reason we don't see giant arthropods anymore is that our atmosphere has less oxygen than it did in the Carboniferous and early Permian periods. There isn't enough oxygen available in your average breath of air to supply a gigantic insect's needs, and the air is too thin to have enough pressure to push the air through all those trachea. Just as a large building needs more air ducts than a smaller one, giant insects require more tracheal tubes than small insects to supply their bodies with air. This means you'll never see an enormous insect capable of knocking down buildings, except in old horror movies.

Breathing Underwater

Some aquatic insect groups have gills as youngsters, and their position on the body varies from family to family. The inside of a dragonfly (Odonata) nymph's hindgut is fitted with tracheal gills; the nymphs swim using jet propulsion from the water they suck up and squirt out of their muscular rear ends, breathing as they squeeze. Mayfly (Ephemeroptera) nymphs and Dobsonfly (Megaloptera) larvae have external abdominal gills, which exchange oxygen and carbon dioxide with the surrounding water. All aquatic insects lose their gills when they leave the water as adults.

Bug Blood

So, do insects have blood? Well, sort of—what passes for blood in insects, centipedes and millipedes is called hemolymph, and, like human blood, it carries digested nutrients absorbed from the gut to the organs and muscles. Bug blood also carries compounds that help clotting and scabbing-over wounds, cells that protect against infection and germs and chemical messages called hormones. Unlike human blood though, hemolymph doesn't carry oxygen or carbon dioxide through the insect's body; the vent-like trachea perform that role.

Bug Bite

Unlike our blood, which is confined to a nice system of arteries and veins, bug blood just sloshes around inside the bug's body. Hemolymph is pumped through the body by a long, tube-shaped heart, called the dorsal aorta, that runs along the inside of the insects' back.

Watch Your Step

When you step on a bug, some of the gunk that shoots out is hemolymph, but most of it is guts, stored fat and other organs. Although getting stepped on is never fun, especially if your guts find their way outside in the process, for the insect, it's not always fatal. Bugs don't have capillaries and other tiny blood vessels like ours that break when we're injured, so sometimes the only serious damage is to the exoskeleton. Because bug blood just sloshes around inside the bug, when it gets squished, the pressure can cause its exoskeleton to break open without any damage to its insides. Guts that spill out through a rupture can sometimes be drawn back inside.

People have told me about stepping on a cockroach in a motel, seeing the guts spill out and assuming they had killed the insect. They later discover that the cockroach has vanished, leaving only a stain where its insides temporarily sat. It's possible that the cockroach merely crawled off to die somewhere else, or it could have been eaten by other cockroaches. But it's also possible that the cockroach survived. Although a ruptured body wall usually leads to death, either by loss of hemolymph or infection, it doesn't always.

Making Sense of it All

Just like us, animals, including insects, have five senses that tell them what's going on in the world and help them find food, shelter and mates and avoid predators and parasites. When it comes to human senses, sight is arguably our most important. Humans have excellent vision, and we're extremely visually oriented. We also see pretty well in colour. This colour vision is the result of three kinds of opsins in the eye, each responsible for detecting a particular wavelength (colour) of light. Though our three opsins see red, green and blue wavelengths, we can distinguish hundreds of thousand shades and colours with our paltry three-opsin system.

Insects have opsins, too, but they see colour differently. Some pollinators, such as bumblebees (Apidae), have a three-opsin system like ours, but, instead of seeing red, blue and green, they see ultraviolet (UV), blue and green. That UV colour reception is useful for pollinating insects that are directed to a flower's nectar by UV markings similar to the airplane landing lights on an airstrip.

Bug Bite

Birds and other reptiles beat
our three opsins with four;
the extra opsin allows them
to see UV light.

UV Attraction

Some crab spiders (Araneae: Thomisidae) have found a
way to make insects' attraction to these UV landing strips
work to their advantage. The Goldenrod crab spider
(*Mitsumena vatia*) appears yellow, white or pink to us; the
colour camouflages the spider as it sits on a flower waiting
for lunch. To bees, flies and other pollinators, however,
the crab spider is a lovely, glowing UV colour, just like the
markings on a nectar-laden flower. In fact, flowers with
crab spiders on them look so good to pollinating insects
that they receive more visits than flowers without. But if
the insect isn't careful, the spider will grab it as it comes
in for a landing.

Colourful Opsins

Some insects, such as butterflies, have as many as five different opsin varieties that allow them to see more shades of almost every colour than humans can. Being able to see many different shades of green can help butterflies find just the right age and type of plants to feed their young. They're looking for healthy plants on which to lay their eggs, so that, when their caterpillars emerge, they will have the best quality of food. Butterflies can also use their impressive colour vision to determine the best flowers to visit—unhealthy or already fertilized flowers have less nectar for the butterfly to drink.

Bug Bite

Butterflies can detect polarity—the direction or slant of light wavelengths. They use polarity to tell them where the sun is, even on a cloudy day, because the light that does get through has a telltale slant to it. Polarity helps species that migrate long distances, such as Monarch and Painted Lady butterflies, know in which direction to travel.

Looks Like Water...

Aquatic insects, such as caddisflies (*Trichoptera*), mayflies and dragonflies, use polarity to find water as they fly around looking for somewhere to lay eggs. These insects recognize a pond or lake, because when light hits the shiny surface, much of it is reflected back with a horizontal polarity. Oddly enough, aquatic insects are often attracted to shiny surfaces with horizontally polarized light—that aren't water at all. They can be tricked by shiny black plastic, oil spills, red and dark-coloured vehicles and the shiny glass windows of buildings near water. Sometimes, at the right time of year, the entire surface of a large office building can be covered in caddisflies. Mayflies will even lay eggs on cars and trucks, because they were mistaken for water. New traps for undesirable species, such as horseflies (Diptera: Tabanidae), could make use of their attraction to these kinds and colours of material.

Seeing Red

The only range of light that insects are not typically sensitive to is infrared. Humans can't see infrared light, either, but we feel it as heat. In fact, our eyes can't detect the far red end of the light spectrum for good reason—the opsins in our eyes would get so hot, they would cook. That's why animals that do sense infrared use special organs not associated with the eyes for the purpose. Rattlesnakes and other pit vipers (Serpentes: Viperidae: Crotalinae) use special pit organs located between the eyes and nostrils to detect heat in the form of infrared.

Pit organs come in handy for some members of the Buprestid family of wood-boring beetles. Because their larvae feed on and burrow through freshly burned wood, the adults must be able to find a recently barbecued tree in which to lay their eggs. The Black fire beetle (Melanophila acuminata) does this not by smell or by sight but by feel, using special pits on the underside of its body to detect the infrared heat trace of forest fires. They will even land on trees that are still hot! Research is currently underway to develop a human infrared sensor that is as simple and as small as a Black fire beetle's for use by fire departments and investigators.

All the Colours of the Rainbow

The award for best vision in the animal kingdom by far goes to an arthropod—but it's not an insect. An order of crustaceans known as the Stomatopoda, or mantis shrimp, have made colour vision an art, thanks to their huge number of opsins! Living in coral reefs and coastal shallows, these crustaceans have used their astounding sight to find well-camouflaged prey for hundreds of millions of years. In addition to their eight receptors for colour (that's one each for the whole rainbow), they can have four devoted just to shades of UV and four for polarity.

Mantis shrimp can tell the difference between light shining down from the water's surface and light that's already bounced off a fish or snail. Add to this compound eyes that can be independently rotated in any direction and that are capable of trinocular depth-perception—the ability to use three points of reference to gauge distance—with only one eye, and you have the best-seeing animal on Earth!

Putting the Ear in Hearing

The ears of crickets and katydids are actually little drum-like tympana on the tibiae, or shins, of the front legs. Grasshoppers have ears on their abdomen. Mantids (the insect order Mantodea, which includes the well-known Praying mantis, *Mantis religiosa*, and more than a thousand others) that fly at night have an ear on their thorax, between the hind legs.

Can You Hear Me Now?

Some insects are very sensitive to sound, especially those that like to make noise. Insects are capable of detecting sound frequencies between 1 and 100,000 Hertz (Hertz means cycles per second); human hearing range is a mere 20 to 20,000 Hertz. That means insects can hear low-frequency sounds that humans can only feel—bass from a stereo subwoofer, for example—and high-pitched sounds well beyond the human auditory range.

Bug Bite

When insects chirp, buzz or produce any kind of stridulation, they're usually looking for mates and advertising their territory. Crickets (Gryllidae) and their cousins, the katydids (Tettigoniidae), sing by rubbing their forewings together; grasshoppers (Orthoptera: Caelifera) sing by rubbing a hind leg against a wing.

Evasive Maneuvers

Other than the odd wing flutter to scare off enemies, mantids do not produce sounds, so they aren't listening for serenading mates; instead, they have an ear out for hungry bats. When a bat lets out a squeak, the sound travels through the darkness and echoes off anything it hits. By interpreting these echoes as insects or objects, the bat can "hear" the shape of its surroundings. This process is called echolocation. When a flying mantid hears the high-frequency shriek of a bat, it will stop flying and drop like a stone or enter into a power dive by banking into a turn and spiralling downward at twice the speed of its normal flight. All these fancy moves make it hard for the bat to track the insect, so the mantid usually escapes.

Many beetles, moths, lacewings (Neuroptera) and orthopterans (grasshoppers, crickets and katydids) are also capable of hearing the ultrasound calls made by hunting bats and will take their own evasive action. This response actually occurs within a few milliseconds of the insect's detection of bat chatter, and by the time the echo even gets back to the bat, the insect has made an escape.

What's That Smell?

Ever wondered why dogs have a better sense of smell than humans? One reason could be the length of our noses. Unlike many dogs, whose noses are long, humans have short faces and short noses, which means there's less room for smell receptors inside the sinuses. A longer nose doesn't always mean a more powerful sense of smell, but the more surface area there is in your sinuses, the more room there is for smell receptors. This can be true of insects. Dragonflies, for example, have tiny, hair-like antennae that are more important for detecting air movement than for smell, and their sense of smell is terrible.

In contrast, males of the giant silk-moth family have huge, feathery antennae capable of detecting a single molecule of the female's pheromone, a long-distance perfume. They have the most potent sense of smell in the animal kingdom!

Feelin' the Vibes

Insects are very sensitive to vibration, thanks to their antennae, legs and the many tiny hairs or spines called setae (singular: seta), which can be located anywhere on the body. These are important in the detection of ground and airborne vibrations, such as wing beats or footsteps. If you look at the back end of a cricket, you'll see a special pair of organs called cerci (singular: cercus). Cerci work like whiskers in mammals, except that they help detect air movement behind the insect. A cockroach can actually feel you approaching as the air underneath your foot compresses and moves out of the way. That's why it's nearly impossible to step on a healthy cockroach.

Leggo My Leg, Bro

Just because insects and other arthropods have a suit of armour doesn't mean they aren't sensitive to changes in that armour. Insects and spiders have highly sensitive structures in their legs that tell them when the exoskeleton is under stress or pressure. If you grab an insect's leg and don't let go, it can tell that something's got hold of it. It can also tell when the leg is being bent the wrong way. An insect can detect even the slightest stresses on its exoskeleton.

Humans are hoping to develop similar stress-sensitive technology for robotics, so that the robots can sense when damage is about to take place or that executing a command like "lift right leg" might actually bend the leg to the breaking point.

We (Don't) Feel Your Pain

No one really knows whether insects can feel pain. Unlike humans, insects apparently lack free nerve endings, which relay information and stresses such as pain. They also lack a neocortex, the part of our mammal brain that's thought to be the site of emotion and pain reception. It's possible, however, that insects might experience nociception. Unlike pain, which is thought to be a conscious experience, nociception is more of an unconscious reflex to avoid damage. When you put your hand on a hot stove, for example, the message zooms up your arm, into your spine and straight to the arm muscles that pull your hand away before your brain even notices that the hand hurts. Being able to detect damage and avoid it is an advantage to any organism.

Although many scientists believe that insects don't feel pain the way we do, genes for nociception have been found in fruit flies. I have watched young mantids get their tarsi (toes) pinched in the lid of their enclosure, and they immediately pulled up the leg to put the injured foot in their mouth. Now it might be that this was a nociceptive, "reflex" response, or that, as predators, mantids will eat anything that smells or tastes like it's bleeding. But it sure looked, to me, like what a human does when he stubs a toe and cradles his foot to ease the pain.

Amazing Bug Abilities

Olympic Sports: Bugs vs Humans

Insects' capabilities are as amazing and varied as they are. Like human athletes, insect record holders have honed their skills over the course of their lives, but they have also inherited traits that kept their parents, their grandparents and their great-grandparents alive.

High Jump: Silver Medal

A human high jumper is a marvel of training and dedication. World records for human jumpers are impressive: Javier Sotomayor of Cuba jumped 2.45 metres (1.25 times his own height) in Salamanca, Spain, in 1993. American Mike Powell leapt 8.95 metres (more than four times his height) to break the world record for long jump in Tokyo, Japan, in 1991.

Sounds impressive (and, for humans, it is), but Sotomayor and Powell have nothing on the humble flea. A flea is the product of natural selection and millions of generations of high jumpers that didn't survive unless they were good at it. Fleas (Siphonaptera) have made jumping a way of life. They didn't bother developing wings; they prefer to leap onto their mammal hosts. The Cat flea (*Ctenocephalides felis*) is capable of jumping 24 centimetres, just high enough to land on the body of a cat. That's 80 times a 3-millimetre adult Cat flea's body length! If I could jump 80 times my body length, I could leap to the top of a 40-storey building. That's more than 140 metres!

High Jump: Gold Medal

A family of insects called froghoppers (Hemiptera: Cercopidae), relatives of aphids and cicadas, make a living by sucking plant juices through their needle-like mouth-parts. Adult froghoppers can fly, but the nymphs, like all immature insects, are wingless. When they're threatened, these guys jump—and, man, can they jump. Take the 6-millimetre-long Common froghopper (*Philaenus spumarius*), for example. Their muscular hind legs lock into the ready-to-jump position, and the leg muscles slowly tighten, storing energy until the legs are released. The legs straighten and the insect is catapulted forward— as far as 70 centimetres at a speed of 4 metres per second. That's a jump of 115 times the common froghopper's body length, edging out the fleas for world's greatest high jumper. To match these guys, our best human jumpers would need to launch themselves 216 metres through the air, higher than a 50-storey building, or high enough to clear the stadium and land in the parking lot!

G-Force Froghoppers

A froghopper's acceleration takes place over a single millisecond, putting a force of as much as 550 gravities (Gs) on the insect. An astronaut heading into space experiences about 5 Gs, and more than 9 Gs will make top fighter-jet pilots lose consciousness. If you happen to see a froghopper up close and decide to poke it to see its world-record jump, I recommend keeping your face clear. If the froghopper hit you in the face, it would feel like being hit with an object 550 times heavier than the insect.

Stings a little.

Bug Bite

We don't really know, for sure, whether the insects mentioned in this section really are the fastest or strongest of all the insects in the world, because we haven't measured all the insects in the world. There are a lot more insects than there are humans or human research scientists—and there are probably even more insects out there that we haven't even discovered yet.

Track and Field

The fastest insects, in terms of absolute speed, are some larger dragonflies, such as the Southern giant darner (*Austrophlebia costalis*) from Australia, which is capable of flying 57 kilometres per hour in short bursts. That's fast enough to get a speeding ticket in a school zone! The fastest human in the world is currently Usain Bolt of Jamaica, who ran 100 metres in 9.69 seconds at the 2008 Olympics in Beijing, China. Although that's more than 10 metres per second, it's only 37 kilometres per hour. The dragonflies would be waiting for him at the finish line.

Fast Feet

Humans would beat any running insect, according to absolute speed. Really, unless it is migrating, an insect rarely runs in any one direction for a kilometre or an hour, so let's consider proportionate speed. Proportionate speed uses an animal's own body length as the measuring stick; this allows us to compare the speed of animals that are different sizes by determining the number of body lengths they can run in a second. Cockroaches are notoriously quick on their feet, and the American cockroach (*Periplaneta americana*) can run 1.5 metres per second—not bad, when you consider that they are about 4 centimetres long. This is only 5.5 kilometres per hour, which wouldn't get them gold in Beijing, but just try to get close enough to one to snap a picture. They can fly even faster, just in case you do catch up with them on foot, so they don't need to be devoted sprinters, at least as adults.

Track and Field: Gold Medal

The fastest runners of all insects are a speedy group of ground beetles called tiger beetles (family Carabidae, subfamily Cincindelinae). Most of them, like the American cockroach and other winged species, run fast and fly even faster, should running down lunch ever become running or flying for your life. Some Australian species of tiger beetles have even lost their ability to fly, in favour of becoming pure sprinters. *Cincindela hudsoni* can run 2.49 metres per second, again, not enough to beat Usain Bolt, but not bad for an animal no more than 2 centimetres long.

However, if we compare those times on a scaled or proportionate speed, where the distance is measured in body lengths, the race might have a different outcome. The speedy tiger beetle is actually covering a distance equal to 120 body lengths per second. Usain Bolt was only travelling about 5.5 body lengths per second to break the world record. If Mr. Bolt wanted to run proportionately as fast as the tiger beetle, he would need to push that 10 metres per second to 216 metres per second, or 777.6 kilometres per hour, enough to break the sound barrier at sea level!

Bug Bite

A smaller Australian tiger beetle, *Cincindela eburneola*, is only about one centimetre long but can run 1.86 metres per second. That's slower than *C. hudsoni* in the absolute sense but a remarkable 171 body lengths per second, which makes this little fellow the fastest land animal, in terms of body size. Although a one-centimetre-long beetle is hardly frightening, just be glad you aren't an ant, the tiger beetle's favourite prey.

Tiger (Beetle) Versus Cheetah

How does the fastest land animal compare to the scaled speed of *C. hudsoni*? The Cheetah (*Acinonyx jubatus*) is rumoured to reach speeds of 80 to 112 kilometres per hour over short distances. With a body length of 1.5 metres (without the tail), in scaled terms, Cheetahs manage about 20 body lengths per second. This works out to an impressive 31 metres per second! However, the proportionate speed pales beside the Australian tiger beetle, which covers 120 body lengths per second. Even the American cockroach, with a speed of 50 body lengths per second, beats the Cheetah.

Impossible Foot Race

Scaled speed is used to estimate which animal would be faster if they were all the same size. If we staged a scenario in which a Cheetah, Usain Bolt, a cockroach and a tiger beetle were all the same body length and had them run a footrace, humans wouldn't even get bronze. Third place would go to the Cheetah, and the insects would take silver and gold. Not only would an oversized tiger beetle break the speed of sound before crossing the finish line, but it also would probably eat the Cheetah and the human on the way past!

Swimming: Gold Medal

Possibly the fastest swimming insects are the whirligig beetles (Gyrinidae). *Dineutes hornii* are capable of speeds up to 0.55 metres per second, not bad for an insect that's only 1.23 centimetres long. That's more than 44.5 body lengths per second. Some whirligigs are thought to be capable of even greater speeds: evidence suggests some species can manage 1.44 metres per second in short bursts.

Whirligig beetles are adapted to live at the water's surface, swimming with their bellies in the water and their backs in the air. Their eyes are evenly divided, so they can see below and above the water at the same time. Whirligigs propel themselves along using their middle and hind pairs of legs, which are short and wide, like canoe paddles. To add to their impressive swimming abilities, whirligig beetles can give off a substance from special pygidial glands in the abdomen that helps propel

them across the water. This surfactant spreads quickly over the surface, pushing the beetles along. Even dead whirligigs are capable of moving 6 centimetres per second across the water. If you want to try this yourself, put a rubber duck or other floating object into a container of water and put a drop of liquid soap or detergent (which acts as the surfactant) behind it. The spreading soap will push the object away.

Bug Bite

Whirligigs turn and twist across the surface of a pond or lake, never travelling in a straight line, even for a second. This is because they actually create waves as they swim and turn; the waves bounce off objects and other insects in the water and return to the beetle. The beetle interprets these wave echoes using ear-like segments in its antennae to avoid collisions with rocks and other beetles and detect potential prey. This behaviour is similar to the echolocation used by bats and dolphins, except that instead of using sound waves, the beetles use water waves.

Impossible Swim Race

At the 2008 Olympics in Beijing, Eamon Sullivan of Australia swam the 50-metre freestyle in 21.28 seconds—that's 2.34 metres, or 1.3 body lengths, per second. Michael Phelps of the United States swam the 200-metre freestyle in one minute and 42 seconds—about 1.96 metres, or a little more than one body length, per second. If you were to put these human record holders in a pool with a whirligig beetle, the beetle would just swim in tight circles and eventually die from chlorine exposure. If they were all the same size, however, the beetle could be capable of swimming 80 metres per second, or 288 kilometres per hour, faster than most speedboats!

Weight Lifting: Gold Medal

When it comes to strength, few people would consider insects worthy of mention. Obviously, we aren't about to hitch insects to a plow or have them move fallen logs, like we would with oxen and Indian elephants. But compared to animals thousands of times their weight, insects are actually quite strong for their size. Rhinoceros beetles (family Scarabaeidae), which are found throughout Asia and South and Central America, are considered the strongest insects of all. These beefed-up beetles are capable of lifting 850 times their own weight! If an elephant bore 850 times its own weight on its back, it would be an elephant pancake! The human equivalent is one person picking up three school buses, full of kids, at the same time. The world's strongest man is currently Mariusz Pudzianowski of Poland, who can lift 395 kilograms, just under three times his own weight. To lift like the rhino beetles, Mr. Pudzianowski would need to lift 112,200 kilograms—more than 112 tonnes.

Bug Bite

Because rhinoceros beetles undergo complete metamorphosis, their adult size is determined by how well fed they were as larvae. The largest males got to be the largest by beating out competitors for food when they were youngsters. Female rhinoceros beetles choose the strongest, toughest males for mates, so they can be sure their offspring will be successful.

Bugs vs the Environment

Insects demonstrate the greatest diversity of shape and lifestyle found anywhere in the animal kingdom, and there are very few places in the world that insects don't call home. The insects' long history has been a story of adaptation to the different conditions found on land and in fresh water, even as they changed significantly.

These Bugs Are Cool

Although you might think that the frozen places of the Earth are devoid of insects, this isn't true. Insects can survive some of the harshest environments on Earth. Sheltered locations within 3° of the North Pole have insect life, and Chironomid midges, a family of flies, can be found in the Antarctic, along with penguin and seal lice (Phthiraptera).

High Fliers

High altitudes and glaciers are not outside of the insect realm; the Himalayan glacier midge (*Diamesa* sp.) can actually fly around actively in air temperatures of -16°C. Ice crawlers (Grylloblattodea), a unique order of insects, are so well adapted to life at high altitudes and cool temperatures that catching one and bringing it down the mountain can cause it to die from heat shock. Preferring temperatures of 1°C or 2°C, they can survive temperatures as low as -6°C; a temperature of 15°C to 20°C is enough to put them into a fatal heat coma. Some midges in Africa, once they have prepared for the dry season by entering a dried-out, dormant state, can tolerate temperatures of −270°C—that's three degrees above absolute zero, the coldest it can get.

Insect Antifreeze

Most insects survive cold temperatures by seeking sheltered, warmer locations, such as under fallen logs or in garages. They can also produce "antifreeze," in the form of sugary alcohols, when the temperatures begin to fall in early winter or late autumn. This antifreeze, which is in the hemolymph and cells, lowers the temperature required to freeze the insect's body solid, usually allowing insects to be alive, though inactive, within a few degrees of zero. Another way insects have adapted to the cold is by transporting water out of their cells and into the body cavity with the hemolymph. Moving the water out of the cells prevents the

cells from bursting when they freeze. Instead, ice crystals form in the body cavity where the water is stored, resulting in less damage to the insect.

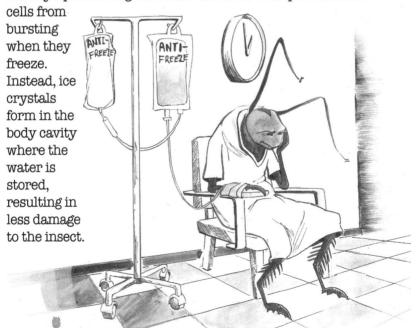

Reverse Raincoat

Insects survive dry environments by waterproofing their outsides. That waxy outer layer of exoskeleton is essentially waterproof—but instead of keeping moisture out, it keeps moisture in. This waterproofing is what allowed insects to be so successful on land so long ago.

Water-resistant skin helps reduce water loss, especially for smaller animals, which are more exposed to the outside environment than larger animals. An elephant's body, for example, has plenty of surface area exposed to the elements, but far more of its body is inside its skin than in contact with the outside environment. An insect's small body size, by comparison, is all within a centimetre or two of its skin, so more of its body is exposed surface area. The exposed surface of an animal loses moisture, so a smaller animal, with its greater degree of exposure, dries out faster and more easily. Waterproofing the exposed area helps insects avoid moisture loss.

Bug Bite

Despite the snow cover, winter is actually a dry time for insects, because available water is locked up as ice and snow. Many insects that can tolerate cold probably adapted their ability to endure drought and the dry season in warmer climates.

Bug Bite

Insects lose moisture when they breathe out, just like humans do. You can see this moisture loss when you exhale on a cold day—the water vapour from your moist breath turns to ice crystals in the air. To prevent moisture loss, insects can close their spiracles (breathing tubes) when their environment is dry.

Holding Water

Some desert insects, such as darkling beetles (Tenebrionidae), have taken waterproofing to the next level. These beetles have an extra-thick cuticle (the waterproof outer layer of exoskeleton), which acts like a reverse raincoat, to keep water in. Their spiracles do not open directly to the outside; instead, they open into the space under their hardened beetle forewings (elytra). The air escapes through the spiracles, but the water is trapped. These beetles' water loss at 30°C is more than 100 times less than that of a suntanning human.

Extreme Water Recycling

Insects that live in the desert don't always have access to drinkable water. So where do they find a drink? Darkling beetles have several adaptations, which work together, to conserve water. The processes of digestion and metabolism create a waste product—water—which is normally disposed of in frass (insect feces) and urine. By absorbing all the water from these processes, darkling beetles "drink" from within their own bodies, making their "pee" a crystalline paste of uric acid, just like the droppings from birds and lizards. They also have a slow metabolic rate, meaning they burn very little energy and require very little food, which reduces water use by the cells and the digestion process.

Darkling beetles are good at storing energy, as well. By giving up the neatly folded wings of other beetles, many darkling beetles have an added site for fat storage. Under their elytra, the fat and all the energy it holds can be saved up for harder times. Like camels, which store energy in the fat of their humps, darkling beetles store their energy under their elytra—and have been doing this since well before there ever were camels. Both groups of animals face the same problems of water and energy conservation, so the solution is the same for both, despite the fact that camels are barely related to beetles at all.

Catching a Drink

Coolest of all the darkling beetles' adaptations is what's called fog basking. Although it might not rain much in the desert, the winds can be humid. Darkling beetles have tiny grooves and pits on the surface of their bodies that act as condensers. When the wind blows, the beetles will stand on a dune, facing the wind with their heads down. As the wind passes over them, their surface structure encourages water droplets to condense in the pits and run down the grooves to form a large drop at the mouth of the beetle. Catching a drink from the wind never looked so easy.

Bug Bite

In dry regions of the Andes Mountains in South America, people are using methods similar to the darkling beetles' to catch moisture from the sea breezes using huge woven nets. They wait for the right time of year, when the wind holds moisture, but not enough to provide rain, then stretch the giant nets across the mountainsides and valleys. When the wind pushes through the nets, it leaves water droplets behind. This is a great idea, but the nets are pretty coarse and let much of the wind and water through without catching anything. By studying the darkling beetles' designs, we might be able to produce far more effective water traps for human use in dry regions of the world.

Long-distance Flying

Migration is the act of moving from one location to another, to avoid nasty weather or to take advantage of better conditions. Some migration is one way, such as when locusts are blown off course to some new region from which they never return. Most migration is two-way, however, such as when Monarch butterflies migrate south for the winter and then turn around and head north again when spring returns. Migration allows animals to take advantage of plentiful food sources during the warm months and to avoid having to cope with winter—when conditions get bad, they just move away.

Amazing Journey

Probably one of the most remarkable migrations regularly made by an insect has to be the annual journey of the Monarch butterfly (*Danaus plexippus*), from Canada and the northern United States east of the Rocky Mountains to the Oyamel forest in Mexico. The migration starts in autumn, when millions of butterflies leave their summer homes and travel south to Mexico's central mountains, a trip that takes about two months. Although the adult Monarch butterfly's lifespan is only about three or four weeks, this special generation, the last of the summer, lives as long as seven or eight months. Once they reach their winter home, they spend three or four months in a deep sleep called torpor, before awakening to mate and begin the return journey northward. They won't make the whole trip, though. As soon as the butterflies have flown far enough north to encounter their only food source, milkweed plants (*Asclepius* spp.), the half-starved butterflies lay their eggs on the plants and die. The caterpillars hatch, eat, grow and pupate quickly in the early Mexican spring, emerging as adults that mate, fly farther north, lay eggs on milkweed plants and then die. This second generation develops and moves farther north, and the process repeats, until three or four generations have passed and the butterflies have reached the northern United States and Canada—it's like a relay race. By this point, summer is winding down, and the days get shorter and cooler. Come fall, the migration begins all over again, with the autumn generation of Monarchs flying all the way to Mexico, just as their great-great-grandparents did, travelling a distance of 2000 to 4500 kilometres from start to finish. This is not only the longest distance ever travelled by an insect but also the largest regular migration of insects.

Bug Bite

The generation of autumn butterflies that lives to eight months and makes the migration to Mexico and part of the way back is called the Methuselah generation. The term refers to a man named in the Bible who apparently lived 969 years, or so the story goes.

Getting Swarmed

Locusts are really just the migrating variety of otherwise normal grasshoppers and behave differently than those born in less-crowded times and places. Migration for them is an adaptation to cope with dwindling food supplies. When conditions are good—say, there's been plenty of rain and enough plants to eat—the well-fed grasshoppers lay more eggs than usual. When the eggs hatch and the young hoppers emerge, they rub shoulders and bump into each other. The more grasshoppers that hatch, the more crowded it gets and the more often they run into each other. When this kind of crowding occurs, the little hoppers produce a pheromone, called gregarization pheromone, which is like a perfume but with a message. The pheromone causes the hoppers to behave as a group—the hopping young and flying adults move together to find food and mates and to migrate to new pastures. Because there are so many of them, they chew through the local food supply pretty quickly. With the food gone, they move on, migrating to stay fed. Once the hoppers reach maturity, the flying adults swarm, spreading out across the countryside looking for more food.

Bug Bite

In 1988, a swarm of Desert locusts (*Schistocerca gregaria*), which are normally found in Africa, the Middle East and western Asia, landed in the West Indies, Surinam and the Guyanas in South America. This means they travelled 4500 kilometres across the Atlantic Ocean—one serious detour for a species! They must have been hungry. Unfortunately, they never made it home to tell their friends.

Amazing Bug Abilities

Vanishing Act

In the 1870s, a swarm of Rocky Mountain locusts (*Melanoplus spretus*) numbering in the trillions darkened the skies of Alberta and the neighbouring U.S. states. They apparently ate every crop in their way, along with clothing hung out to dry, wooden handles from farming implements and even the leather off boots. Although the Rocky Mountain locust was a regular scourge across the Prairies, in 1902, they vanished. We don't know for sure what caused the vanishing act, but it's thought that something occurred in the locusts' home range—which must have been a protected area with abundant resources—to allow the grasshoppers to reach the densities necessary for migratory behaviour. This area might have been developed or logged, inadvertently destroying the locusts' home range. Unfortunately, although the farmers were probably happy that the locusts were gone, species such as the Burrowing owl (Strigidae: *Athene cunicularia*) lost their periodic locust buffet. In fact, because of dwindling food supplies, a lack of habitat and chronic exposure to insecticides, Burrowing owls are now considered endangered in Canada.

Bug Bite

The biggest locust swarms occur in desert regions of Africa, the Middle East and Western Asia. Sometimes measured from airplanes, multiple swarms covering 1000 square kilometres, with probably 500 billion insects overall, have been sighted. If humans were to turn the tables on locusts and eat them, we could probably feed the hungry, avoid the need for insecticides and make the farmers happy at the same time. Locust burgers, anyone?

Insect Survival Skills

Part of every organism's survival arsenal is the ability to defend itself from attack. Even plants have clever ways to avoid being eaten—like sprouting spines and carrying toxins. If they're threatened, insects, like most animals, will hide or run away before they'll put up a fight. But some insects defend themselves in bizarre and interesting ways.

Explosive Insect

Bombardier beetles are accomplished explosives technicians. A member of the ground beetle family (Carabidae), bombardier beetles have paired glands in their abdomen; one gland contains chemicals such as hydrogen peroxide (used in bleach and hobby rocket fuel); in the other gland is peroxidase. When threatened, the beetle squeezes the hydrogen peroxide through the chamber with the peroxidase, combining them in the process. This chemical reaction produces irritating chemicals that explode out of the beetle's back end at almost 100°C! Some species can even swivel their abdomens to shoot the concoction in any direction. The would-be predator is sprayed with a boiling mixture of gas and liquid chemicals that can burn human skin and even kill insect attackers.

Better Than Scuba Gear

Unless they're in a submarine, most people use scuba gear to explore coral reefs up close. One major drawback to this system is the finite air supply contained in the tanks. Aquatic insects have been living in water, despite the fact that many still breathe air, for millions of years. Some have developed functioning gills, but others rely on special waterproof hairs that trap air bubbles. Predaceous diving beetle adults (Dytiscidae), water bugs (Belostomatidae) and backswimmers (Notonectidae) carry air bubbles when swimming and diving under the water's surface.

If the bubble worked like a scuba setup, they would run out of oxygen in a few seconds; after all, the bubble can only hold so much air. A larger bubble would hold more air and therefore more oxygen, but the insect would be fighting the buoyancy of the bubble and would waste precious oxygen trying to stay submerged.

Why is a plain old bubble better than scuba gear? Because it is not self-contained—the bubble actually "breathes" by itself. As the insect uses up oxygen in the bubble, more diffuses in from the surrounding water. The carbon dioxide that the insect breathes out diffuses through the bubble into the water around it. As the insect dives deeper, the pressure on the bubble increases, causing the new oxygen to move into the air space faster. The bubble doesn't last forever, though; eventually the other gases in the air bubble are absorbed by the water, and the insect must return to the surface for a new one.

Can't Beat a Good Design

Cockroaches (Blattodea) might be some of the most reviled animals of all time, but, even if you don't like them, you should probably respect them. Cockroaches are survivors. Over more than 300 million years of evolution, the cockroach has changed very little; like the Great white shark, it settled on a timeless design early on. Our disgust for cockroaches stems from finding them in our homes, garbage dumps and sewers, whether we want them there or not. They're good at finding rotting vegetable, fruit, fungus and animal matter and disposing of it the best way they know how: by eating it. To be fair, only about 30 species actually benefit from human activity, and only 12 of those will live in your house. That leaves another 4270 cockroach species that mind their own business and don't deserve to be called pests.

Rad Resistance

Cockroaches are known for their resistance to radiation, leading to the popular belief that they will inherit the Earth after humans make a nuclear wasteland of the place. This is not entirely false, but even metal evaporates if it's close enough to ground zero of your average atomic explosion, in which air temperatures reach that of the sun's surface. Even resilient cockroaches would not survive that kind of insult. They are, however, capable of tolerating much higher levels of radiation than humans and other animals.

How tolerant are they? House-pest species, such as the German, Brown, Oriental and American cockroaches, have been shown to tolerate 83 to 110 times the amount of radiation that would kill a human in one dose. How do they manage this? Actually, there is nothing special about the roaches on this count. Other insects, such as beetles, can survive similar levels of radiation. DNA gets damaged by radiation when it is being read and copied. If a cell wants to grow or divide, it must open up the stored DNA for building instructions or to make copies. When the DNA is open, it's no longer safely packaged and can be hit by radiation, which causes mistakes in the reading and copying. These mistakes are called mutations, and they are usually bad for the organism.

Our cells are constantly opening our DNA, which is normally twisted and bundled into safe packages for storage in the nuclei, the library and control centres of most cells. But because most insects only grow during moulting, their DNA is safely stowed in their nuclei the rest of the time. When it is all wound up into dense bundles, the DNA is protected from all but the highest levels of radiation.

Another reason we're more susceptible to radiation poisoning is that our skin is pretty thin and transparent, compared to insect exoskeleton, so it lets more radiation through to our cells and their DNA. A moulting cockroach would be just as susceptible to radiation poisoning as a human—its soft exoskeleton wouldn't shield it, and, because it's growing, its open, unprotected DNA can be damaged, leading to mutations. So, cockroaches not busy moulting would survive much closer to the site of an atomic blast than any humans. But they would still need to moult eventually. To survive, they would need to find an area with low enough levels of radiation to carry on life as usual.

Losing Your Head

Most people know that a cockroach can live without a head, but did you know they can live without one for as long as 14 days? They can do this because of the layout of their nervous system. Cockroaches and other insects have a brain in the head, but they also have several nerve clusters, called ganglia (singular: ganglion), that act like tiny brains for each segment of the body. With no head, the ganglia in the thorax each move their own pair of legs, and those in the abdomen work the breathing muscles and guts, so the rest of the body goes on without it.

Now you might think: "can't they moult and just grow a new head?" The answer is no. Glands in the brain secrete the hormones that control moulting, so a headless roach would not be able to grow a new one. Perhaps the strangest thing about decapitated cockroaches is that they still run away from light. This means they must be able to detect bright light, or possibly the heat from the light, through the exoskeleton, because their eyes are still with the disembodied head.

Bug Bite

Because humans keep the vital parts of the nervous system in our heads, we can't live long without them. Evidence suggests that humans have at least a few seconds of awareness after our heads are removed, but we certainly can't roam around for two weeks, like roaches can.

Record Holders

Insects' bodies are varied in shape and function, thanks to their diverse lifestyles. Some insects are worthy of mention because they are record holders within the class Insecta; others are contenders for records within all of the animal kingdom. Here are some insects that belong in the insect and animal halls of fame.

Longest Tongue

The vast majority of moths and butterflies (Lepidoptera) have special coiled mouthparts designed for siphoning nectar from flowers. These proboscides, or proboscises (singular proboscis), can be straightened out by a combination of blood pressure and special muscle action. In 1862, Charles Darwin, the father of evolutionary biology, had the opportunity to contemplate a monster tongue when he examined a Malagasy star orchid from Madagascar. The flowers have no area to land on and must be pollinated by visitors capable of hovering. To make things even more difficult for any interested insect, the nectar is housed in a 30-centimetre-long spur that juts from the back of the flower.

When Darwin saw this, he reasoned that this flower must be pollinated by a sphinx moth with an equally long proboscis. Why a sphinx moth? Sphinx moths (Sphingidae) are strong fliers and are more than capable of hovering at an orchid with no landing strip. Darwin was ridiculed at the time; after all, there was no sphinx moth with a proboscis that long. In 1903, however, Morgan's Madagascan sphinx moth (*Xanthopan morganii praedicta*) was discovered—and, yes, it had a tongue almost as long as the flower spur. Darwin was already dead by then, but no doubt he knew his hypothesis was correct, despite the jeers of his colleagues.

Lightest on Their Feet

Possibly the lightest animals on their feet are the water striders (Gerridae), which are capable of walking on the surface of ponds and sloughs. Striders have this ability because they can trap air in their waterproof leg hairs, which then act like buoys. They still need to be very light-weight, however, so they can stand on the surface tension of the water without falling through. Their tarsi (toes) have claws that actually grip the water's surface, so they can row around the pond looking for unlucky insects that have fallen in.

Bug Bite

Extremely tiny insects called Thrips (Thysanoptera) are so lightweight that flying through the air is, for them, more like swimming. They have fringed wings that look more like feather dusters than those of most insects. Because they are so small (most are less than 1 millimetre), they are not powerful fliers but can be carried great distances by the wind.

Fastest Flappers

As the first animals to fly, insects are arguably the most well-adapted flyers out there. They also win the prize for being the fastest flappers. Hummingbirds can flap their wings anywhere from 10 to 200 beats per second (bps). Butterflies are capable of 10 bps, dragonflies manage around 35 bps and bees can pull 130 bps. Flies, as their name suggests, are the most impressive flappers, though. Houseflies buzz at about 170 bps, and mosquitoes whine with their wings beating at 600 bps. But the record goes to the midges, which are capable of more than 1000 bps!

Largest War Party

The biggest insect army is a toss-up between the South American army ants (*Eciton* spp.) and the African driver ants (*Dorylus* spp.), which live in colonies of as many as 20 million. As daughters of the same queen, the ants are all sisters, and the colonies work together more like a single super-organism than millions of individuals. Hunting, nest building and babysitting are all taken care of by closely related sisters.

In case you were wondering, it's never a good idea to start a fight with social insects, such as ants or wasps. Even if you only kill a single offending wasp or ant, you could be in trouble: the dying bug releases an attack pheromone, and, if you're too close to the colony, it will alert her sisters. If you've squashed an army or driver ant, better run—ant raiding parties can number 500,000.

An Army of Cleaners

In Costa Rica, locals recommend you leave for a couple of hours if army ants happen to pass through your home. Upon your return, you will be pleasantly surprised to find that they have cleaned your house for you. There won't be so much as a leg, wing or crumb left after the ants have captured, butchered and carried off any of your former insect or spider roommates. Larger animals can safely flee, unless tethered; usually, it's the invertebrates and smaller frogs and lizards that are unable to escape in time.

Deepest Dweller

Thanks to human ingenuity—and manned and remote control submarines—land-dwelling, air-breathing humans have found ways to explore the vast, unknown depths of the ocean. Without a submarine, however, we don't come close to reaching the depths enjoyed by *Hirondellea gigas*, a shrimp-like Amphipod crustacean. This crustacean survives on particles of food that rain down from shallower areas of the ocean into the Pacific Ocean's Mariana Trench, 11 kilometres below sea level. If a human scuba diver tried to dive to this depth, he would be crushed under the pressure of the seawater. The deepest confirmed scuba dive by a human is a mere 318 metres (that's 0.318 kilometres), achieved by Nuno Gomez in the Red Sea in 2005.

Longest Insect

The world's longest insect is the Malaysian giant stick insect (*Phobaeticus serratipes*), which can reach a leg span of 55.5 centimetres! That's more than half a metre of insect. These gangly vegetarians even have a 3-centimetre leg span when they hatch from their eggs, which seem much too small for the leggy youngsters. This is because many insects will moult as they hatch, growing as they emerge. In fact, although they were folded like origami within the egg, by the time we see them out of their eggshells, they have already had a growth spurt.

Smallest Insect

The smallest insect in the world is a parasitoid wasp called *Dicopomorpha echmepterygis* (Mymaridae), a.k.a. the Fairy fly. Fairy flies lay their eggs inside the eggs of another group of insects called bark lice (Psocoptera:

Psocidae). Obviously, an insect has to be very small to hijack the eggs of other insects. The males of this species are wingless and tiny, only 139 micrometres long (though females are larger)! That's 0.139 millimetres, smaller than a single-celled amoeba or Paramecium, such as those you find in a drop of pond water and can only see under a microscope. The Fairy flies' tiny size permits a sneaky lifestyle: they fly about, locating bark louse eggs using their sense of smell, and then tiptoe in close enough to inject their own eggs.

Bug Bite

To be considered a parasite, an organism must live on or in another being (the host) and cause harm to it. If the organism is guaranteed to kill the host in the process, then it's a parasitoid.

Smallest Insect Eggs

The smallest insect eggs are not Fairy fly eggs; the smallest insect eggs belong to a family of flies called Tachinids. Approximately 8000 species of Tachinidae can be found around the world, and most are parasitoids, meaning their larval development takes place inside or on insect hosts. The female either lays its eggs on the host and lets the hatched larvae burrow inside on their own, or she injects them directly into the host. She might even leave them where the unwitting host will eat them. Inside the host, the larvae devour the body, starting with the least important parts, so the host will live as long as it takes for the maggots to become flies. Some Tachinid eggs are only 20 micrometres long—0.02 millimetres. That's seriously tiny.

Longest Living

The longest-living insect is a category with a few contenders. Queen ants (Formicidae), collected as already mated adults, have lived for more than 28 years in captivity. Two families of wood-boring beetles, the longhorn (Cerambycidae) and metallic borers (Buprestidae), spend their larval development inside wood. Sometimes, if the wood is extremely dry and has little nutritional value, the larvae can take decades to reach adulthood. Now and then, the larvae are accidentally processed into lumber when the trees they inhabit are cut down and made into building material, or the adult females lay their eggs in already processed lumber, and the larvae begin to eat the wood.

These beetles have emerged from boards in the walls of homes, banisters and antique furniture more than 50 years after construction! It's difficult to tell whether these wood-boring beetles are older than the furniture from which they emerged, or if they found their way into the wood after it was processed. Both are possible. Although this is an impressive feat, wood-boring beetles don't typically develop this slowly; if the wood they eat is of high quality, they can reach adulthood in only a few years.

Bug Bite

Although they aren't insects, some desert tarantulas (Araneae: Theraphosidae) can live for several decades. Male tarantulas are short-lived, usually surviving three to six years, but females typically outlive their brothers significantly. Female Mexican red-kneed tarantulas (*Brachypelma smithi*) have been known to live for 50 years!

Most Offspring from One Egg

Given the ridiculous number of insects in the world, they must have plenty of offspring. Some have many all at once, and others spread it out over their entire lives. A brood is a single batch of young, produced by one set of parents, that all emerge at the same time. A typical human brood, for example, consists of one child, although sometimes it's two, if they are twins, or three, if they are triplets. Human identical twins are the result of one embryo developing into two individuals. The process in some parasitoid wasps in the family Encyrtidae is the same, with one major exception—one egg can actually hatch into 3000 individual wasp larvae, all hungry and ready to dine on the insides of their hosts. These tiny wasps parasitize everything from aphids to caterpillars, which makes them important pest-control agents.

Most Offspring: Social Insects

African driver ant (*Dorylus* spp.) queens are capable of laying three to four million eggs every 25 days! Part of the reason the queen ant needs to continually lay so many eggs is that her daughters, the workers and soldiers that do all the legwork in the massive colony, are not especially long-lived. For the social Hymenoptera (bees, wasps and ants living in colonies), worker lifespan is measured more accurately in mileage than in time. The farther they venture to forage, or the harder they fight prey and enemies, the shorter their lives will be. A queen ant must replenish her workforce by laying eggs throughout her adult life or risk having to do all the housework herself.

Bug Bite

One Australian ghost moth (Hepialidae) observed in a laboratory laid 29,000 eggs and was found to have another 15,000 fertilized eggs still inside her. Presumably, she was taking a break between sets.

Most Offspring Per Year

Aphids are yet another remarkable family (Aphididae) capable of reproducing asexually, which is to say, all by themselves without a mate. When the plants they feed on are healthy and the weather is warm, female aphids give birth to identical daughters that are already pregnant!

Every 10 days, she can produce another daughter (or 10) with babies inside her, which have babies inside them. If each of her daughters has daughters of her own every 10 days, and they have daughters of their own and so on, one female aphid could produce more than six billion offspring in one year! If a population of aphids were to have a 100-percent-survival rate for one year, the resulting millions of tons of aphids would weigh twice that of the world's entire human population and could stretch

single-file around the world at the equator four times!

Fortunately, for the plants the aphids feed on, and the farmers, gardeners and forestry workers who rely on those plants, aphids have plenty of predators. Thanks to the lacewings (Neuroptera) and ladybugs (Coccinellidae) that eat them, the parasitoid wasps that lay eggs inside them and the seasonal weather that turns their food into dry twigs, they never get so numerous.

Largest Human Families

The most children born at once were decaplets (10!), to a mother in Brazil in 1946. The record for most babies from one mother goes to Feodor Vassilyev's unnamed first wife, who had 69 children between 1725 and 1765. As someone who gave birth 27 times, to 16 sets of twins, seven sets of triplets and four sets of quadruplets, her name really ought to have gone down in history. It didn't. The most children ever had by a single father goes to the former king of Swaziland, Sobhuza II, who had 70 wives and 210 children. Perhaps he had an eye on more than one world record, because he is also the most prolific grandpa, with more than 1000 grandchildren. Although this is certainly impressive, it's safe to say he had an easier time of it than Mrs. Vassilyev did.

Bug Bite

Even the largest human families pale in comparison to 20 million driver ant sisters born to one mother. Because the male ants die shortly after mating, queen ants deserve respect for being the world's most successful single mothers.

Most Moults

Most insects moult as juveniles and then cease when they reach adulthood. Sometimes unusually large species increase the number of moults they go through as youngsters, compared to their smaller relatives, to reach their adult size. Instead of bulking up with a few huge moults, they grow a manageable size with each moult and simply go through more of them. Some of the more primitive insect groups, such as the bristletails and silverfish, keep moulting, even as adults. Mayflies (Ephemeroptera) do stop moulting once they reach adulthood, which only lasts about an hour, but they can moult 45 times over the two or three years they take to reach that point. The bristletails might moult as many as 60 times in a lifetime, which is enough to beat the 50-year-old, female Mexican red-kneed tarantulas, to take first place in the most-lifetime-moults category.

Most Venomous

Surprisingly, the most potent insect venom isn't from a hornet or Africanized bee; it belongs to the Harvester ant (Formicidae: *Pogonomyrmex maricopa*). Harvester ants can sting in defense and deliver venom with a lethal dose of 0.12 milligrams per kilogram, meaning 12 stings is enough to kill a 2-kilogram rat. Humans experience four hours of intense pain from a single sting. This system of milligrams of venom per kilogram of animal being stung doesn't always take into account that some kinds of venom are more effective on some animals than on others. Most venom experiments involve lab mice, which are close enough to humans to give us an idea of how we might react. Based on this kind of data, those Harvester ants have more potent venom than all but the 10 most-dangerous snakes (mostly taipans and sea snakes).

Insect Occupations

Insect Architects

Insects, as you might imagine, make homes in quite a variety of shapes and sizes, from many different kinds of materials. The most impressive homes are those that house millions of related occupants—for example, the nests of social insects such as termites and ants. Their success lies in the division of labour. Workers, because of the number of them, can feed larvae, repair the nest, forage for food and defend against predators—all at the same time. This is far more efficient than performing each task one after the other, like a solitary animal must. In regions where it is warm year round, social insects can maintain nests that might be decades old.

Keeping Cool

Some African termite mounds are specially designed to ventilate themselves; in effect, they have air conditioning—but in a greener way than our human version, because it doesn't require any energy except for construction and maintenance. Air is circulated by a complex system of tunnels that act as air vents, cooling the air as it comes close to the mound surface. This not only provides cooler air but also gets rid of carbon dioxide and brings in fresh oxygen, as air rises in the central chimney and sinks in the outer tunnels. The entire system is constructed using only mud and saliva, sculpted by the 2-centimetre-long termite (Isoptera: Termitidae) workers. Why build such an exquisite climate-control system?

To maintain the perfect temperature and carbon dioxide levels to farm fungus in the cellar, of course. Not only are the termites great architects, they are farmers, too.

Solar Heating

In Australia, termites have built mounds 6 metres tall and oriented like a blade or a shark's dorsal fin, so the thin edges point north and south, and the flat sides face east and west. Some refer to these as "magnetic" mounds, because of their alignment with compass directions. As the sun rises, light hits the east face of the mound and warms it up. The west face at this point is still in the shade and is still cool. By noon, the sun is so hot, it would scorch the termite mound—except that the mound's narrowest aspect is the top, which means that the high, overhead sun shines on only a thin portion of the termite's home during the hottest part of the day. As afternoon hits, the sun heats the west side of the mound, leaving the east face to cool in the shade. Because the surface of the mound is porous, the wind passing over the mound blows away the hot air from inside the colony and brings in fresh, cool air.

Termite Towers

Compared to buildings constructed by humans, termite mounds are more efficient and easier to build, and they're made of biodegradable natural materials. A 6-metre-tall termite mound holding a few million inhabitants, each only 2 centimetres long, is equivalent to a human high-rise of at least 180 stories. When Dubai's 160-storey Burj Dubai is completed, it will be the tallest building in the world. You can bet it won't have a few million human residents, and it sure won't have wind-powered air conditioning, either.

Green Design

Insects can create some truly sophisticated architecture with natural materials. Wasp nests range from insulated, papier-mâché hives to beautifully sculpted mud-and-clay pots. Spiders weave webs that have inspired humans for thousands of years; using their own silk secretions, spiders can build homes, snares, egg cases and even nets that can be stronger than steel of the same thickness. Insects produce silk, too—not just caterpillars but also some larval bees, wasps and ants; caddisflies (Trichoptera); adult web spinners (Embioptera) and even male bristletails (Archaeognatha). Silk is used for building a safe place to pupate (undergo metamorphosis to become adult) and to stitch together a protective case in which to live and even mate.

Caddisfly Carpenters

Caddisfly (Trichoptera) larvae live in rivers, ponds and lakes, where they spend most of their time rooting around for small plants or animals to eat. The larvae build cases out of any materials they can find: sand, stones and wood, for example, which they carry around with them. They even put it all together with their own silk. The cases help camouflage the slow-moving youngsters against the bottom of the pond or river. Even larvae kept in an aquarium will use available items, such as beads, gems, pearls and even plastic garbage, to disguise their portable homes. It is not uncommon to see a wild individual with the odd piece of brightly coloured plastic or rusty fishing lure incorporated into its case.

Guests with Gall

Perhaps the trickiest of all insect architects are the gall-forming wasps (Cynipidae), flies (Cecidomyiidae) and bugs (Hemiptera: Aphididae, Adelgidae, Psyllidae). Females laying eggs are very careful about where they put them. Often they are left on or inside of a leaf, twig or stem of the appropriate host plant. Then the larvae, either by feeding at certain sites, or even releasing hormones that fool the plant into growing differently, allow their host to build a home for them.

When a gall midge (Diptera: Cecidomyiidae) larva enters a plant, the plant tries to seal it up, by surrounding the parasite with tough, woody tissue that we call a gall, hoping to trap it and minimize damage from it. The end result is a safe, little "house" for the parasite. As if that weren't enough, gall-forming insects have found ways of convincing their hosts to grow complex systems of veins within the gall; the veins provide the larvae with a rich and steady supply of delicious plant juices!

To recap: the insect breaks into the plant's body, the plant tries to trap it and the insect tricks the plant into providing meals on tap—the parasite has effectively had an impenetrable fortress of living tissue, complete with stocked larder, built for it by its host. Once the gall-forming insects are mature, they usually leave the gall, and, after finding mates, they will lay more eggs on plants, which will result in more galls.

Farmers and Ranchers

Although humans probably assume that we were the first animals to farm, we weren't: insects were farming long before we were. How do we know this? By studying fossils and insects trapped in amber. Scientists can determine how long fungus-farming ants have been farmers by comparing differences between the DNA of modern-day ant farmers and non-farming ants and the DNA of farmed fungus and related wild fungus. Leaf-cutter ants and their relatives have been farming for at least 60 million years—that's more than 59 million years longer than humans have!

Old Hands

Insect and human farming probably started out in the same way: foods preferred by gatherers (plants for humans, fungus for insects) would have sprouted up where the seeds and spores were left on garbage heaps and outdoor toilets. Once the plants or fungus started to grow, the gatherers used a little maintenance to keep less-desirable "weeds" from competing with the crop—and, voilà, they were farming.

Some ants and termites farm fungus within their nests, where they can control the conditions to encourage growth. The termite-farmed fungus grows naturally on termite frass (insect poop), supporting the theory that food grows first in garbage dumps and refuse piles. Insect livestock farming might have begun as simple foraging for the right kinds of insects and then developed into herding, as the insect farmers took to moving their flocks to new pastures, instead of having to find new insect cattle every time the host plant dies.

Ant Gardens

Plant- and seed-feeding ants sometimes alter their environment by collecting and eating the seeds of undesirable plants and leaving the desirable seeds to germinate. In some forests, ant-engineered meadows containing only the favoured plants are known locally as "Devil's gardens," the name given by people who could only imagine one explanation for why some areas of the forest grew only one type of plant, when others grew a variety of them: it must be the work of Satan. In fact, it was the work of ant colonies, but the people didn't know that. Of course, ants are no more evil than human gardeners pulling weeds. It is through sheer work effort, and not through the use of chemicals, that ants succeed in their own brand of weed control.

Fungus Farmers

Some termites (Isoptera), such as the African species *Macrotermes natalensis*, farm fungus, as do many ant species. Leaf-cutter ants (Formicidae: *Atta* spp. and *Acromyrmex* spp.) feed on the fruiting bodies of their farmed fungus and must supply the fungus with fresh-cut leaves and a stable environment for it to grow. They need to weed out pest fungi and are helped by bacteria that grow on their bodies and secrete special antibiotic substances, which kill off the unwanted fungi. A new queen leaving the nest will tuck a wad of fungi, enough to start a garden that will feed a colony of her own, into a pocket in her mouth before she goes.

Aphid Ranching

Ants culture their own insect livestock, usually aphids (Hemiptera: Aphididae) or scale insects (Coccoidea), which spend their days sucking the juices out of plants. Ants do not slaughter their herd; instead, they feed on the sugary liquid that the bugs produce, called honeydew. The honeydew is the byproduct of a high-sugar, liquid diet that the aphids and scale insects survive on and then excrete (like we do if we drink too many glasses of pop). Some species are capable of producing their own weight in honeydew per day, so there's plenty for the ants. The ants "milk" their insect cattle for honeydew by gently caressing them with their antennae.

If the plants feeding the ant's flock start to die, an aphid cattle drive ensues. The ants pick up their herd members, one by one, and carry them to greener pastures—other plants. It's possible that this relationship was established by the time the dinosaurs disappeared, 65 million years ago, well before anything resembling a cow, goat or even human appeared.

Getting
Along

You Scratch My Back, I'll Scratch Yours

Mutualism is a cooperative relationship that benefits both partners. These partnerships might have developed from an initially unfriendly interaction, in which one organism benefited and the other did not. Over time, the exploited party adapts to prevent the other organism from taking advantage of it, and a working relationship is forged. It's also possible that some partnerships might have been fair and equal from the start, but this is probably less common. Relationships that benefit one participant and neither harm nor help the other are called commensal.

Three-way Partnership

Flowering plants and pollinating insects have hammered out a relationship that benefits more than the plant and the insect. The flowers provide nectar to hungry insects, and, in return, the insects spread pollen from one flower to the next, ensuring that the flowers bear seeds that will develop into the next generation of plants. In turn, this pollination helps crop production.

Bug Bite

Sometimes, one of the partners in a plant-insect partnership cheats—the plant being pollinated fails to live up to its obligation and doesn't provide a nectar meal to the pollinator, or the insect steals nectar without pollinating the flower.

Bee Kind to Bees

The European honeybee (*Apis mellifera*) performs most of the pollination that occurs in our modern human agricultural system. In fact, thanks to the honeybee, humans are growing crops in parts of the world where natural pollinators for these crops don't exist. Unfortunately, this isn't a good thing: the simpler the system (fewer species of plants, animals and other organisms), the more susceptible to disturbance and disaster it is. If we were to lose the honeybees—which are suffering from a number of parasites and diseases these days—an estimated 90 percent of our fruit, seed and nut crops would fail! By growing acres and acres of the same crops—orchards, fields and plantations—we lose the natural meadows and patches of wild flowers that are habitats for a wealth of native pollinating insects.

Much Obliged

Perhaps the most impressive pollinator-plant relationship is that of the soapweed (*Yucca glauca*), or yucca, and the Yucca moth (Prodoxidae: *Tegeticula yuccasella*). The yucca's flowers open at night, when the moths are active. Female Yucca moths collect pollen from the flowers and carry it to the next flower or plant. So far, it's not much different from the average pollinator-plant relationship, right? Here's where it gets weird. When the female moth gets to the next flower, she makes a hole in the wall of the flower's ovary and lays a single egg inside. After that, she climbs up to the stigma, the opening of the flower's female part, and stuffs her collected pollen in. By doing this, she ensures that the flower develops a healthy number of seeds—which just happen to be what her caterpillar children eat.

This kind of relationship is called obligate, because the moth and plant are obliged to work together—no other moth will pollinate these flowers, and no other plant can provide the necessary nursery. The soapweed tolerates having some seeds eaten by hungry Yucca moth caterpillars; in turn, the caterpillars don't eat all the seeds. If they did, it wouldn't be such a good deal for the plant. However, the coolest part of all is the plant's ability to prevent being cheated. If too many female Yucca moths visit a flower, which would mean having too many, or even all, of the developing seeds eaten, the plant simply drops that flower and its moth eggs. The soapweed can then concentrate on developing seeds in less-popular flowers.

Teaming Up, Forever

Sometimes cooperative relationships work so well that the partner organisms permanently join forces, and neither is found without the other. This is called symbiosis, which means "living together," and the partners are called symbionts. For example, most termites are symbiotic with the tiny primitive protozoa that live in their guts and help break down the wood fibre that makes up the termite diet. For the fungus-farming termites, the fungus is responsible for breaking down plant fibre, which explains why the termites need to build such elaborate mounds to maintain exactly 30°C, unwavering humidity levels and the right soil acidity for fungus growth.

Little Houses

Some plants actually encourage ants to live inside them—
they produce special hollow stems, roots, leaves and
thorns for the ants, called domatia, or little houses. Known
as myrmecophytes, which means ant-plants, these plants
grow domatia whether ants are around or not. The ants
usually chew a hole through the wall of the specially built
ant apartment to gain access and then take up residence.
To prevent injury to the plant, while still providing low-
effort housing to the ants, the domatia typically have an
easily chewed access point that heals quickly.

What does the plant get out of the arrangement? By
providing the ants with shelter, and sometimes nectar
and other nutritious liquids, the plants receive benefits
in return. The ants protect their host plant by attacking
plant-eating insects and large plant-eating mammals and
by pruning away harmful vines that would otherwise
strangle their living home. Ant tenants
more fiercely defend plants that
provide the best shelter, nectar
and other food.

Helpful Hand-me-downs

All termites are social, living in colonies and working together through all stages of development. Living in a colony might be the only way for young and recently moulted termites to obtain a steady supply of protozoa, through trophallaxis, the act of regurgitating or pooping out fluids of the digestive system to share with others. As workers feed each other and the younger generations, some of the gut protozoa are passed along, which is how the termites acquire the symbionts that they cannot live without. Those gut protozoa have been handed down, one termite to the next, for millions of years!

Gang Warfare

The Mountain pine beetle (Curculionidae: Scolytinae: Dendroctonus ponderosae) is a tiny fellow in the weevil family that feeds on dying trees too weak to defend themselves. The beetles do this by first overwhelming the tree's defenses—the sticky sap. Here's how it works: if a single Mountain pine beetle bores into the trunk of a lodge pole pine, the tree bleeds sap, which either ejects the beetle or seals it in a sticky tomb. But if thousands of beetles attack en masse, the tree doesn't have enough sap and is too full of holes to effectively defend itself against the bugs. To get the gang together, beetles send out what's called an aggregation pheromone—kind of like a long-distance perfume that serves as a party invitation—and coordinate an attack by many of the beetles in the area on a single tree.

Fungus Among Us

Special pits on the Mountain pine beetle's mouthparts contain a fungus known as Blue-stain (Ophiostoma sp.). Once the beetle is inside the tree's soft tissue (called the cambium) beneath the bark, the fungus starts to spread. As it grows, it clogs up the tree's xylem and phloem, the veins that carry water and nutrients, choking the tree to death. In fact, the spreading fungus does more damage to the tree's defenses than the actions of the beetles themselves. The beetles' purpose in attacking the tree is to lay eggs that will hatch into hungry larvae that love to eat freshly dead cambium. When this new generation of beetles has fed, grown and pupated inside the dead tree, they feed on the fungus and emerge with their own bundle of Blue-stain fungus tucked into their mouthparts, ready to turn it loose on the next tree.

Bug Bite

Wood infected with the Blue-stain fungus has been marketed as designer "denim-wood," for its blue colour.

Working within the System

The Mountain pine beetle has wrought havoc in managed forests and national parks across British Columbia and Alberta. The beetles, which are native to our forests, attack mostly older trees (those 80 to 125 years old). Their role is to kill off older stands of trees and make way for new growth, much as forest fires do. When a pine beetle outbreak occurs, we have to find ways to log the forests so we can use those older trees before either the beetles or forest fires get them first.

Not wanting our forests to burn has left many more old trees standing than would survive if forest fires were allowed to happen naturally. Because old trees are the beetle's favourite, we have unwittingly laid out a buffet for them. To help reduce the pine beetle infestation and prevent them in the future, new forest management practices need to include more planned fires (called prescribed burns) and earlier harvesting of aging trees. Replanting with several different tree species of different ages can also prevent similar problems in the future.

Eaten from Inside

Certain parasitoid wasps practice a creepy kind of symbiosis. First, these wasps seek out a living host, usually a caterpillar, aphid or spider. After stinging the host to momentarily disable it, the wasp injects its eggs and a special virus into the helpless host. The virus disables the host's immune system, so it can't fight off the wasp larvae. When the eggs hatch inside, the larvae begin to eat the living tissues, starting with the least important. Eventually, the wasp larvae get enough to eat and either pupate within the host or chew their way out to become adults elsewhere. This kills the host, but the new generation of wasps also has its own supply of the virus to use on the next victim.

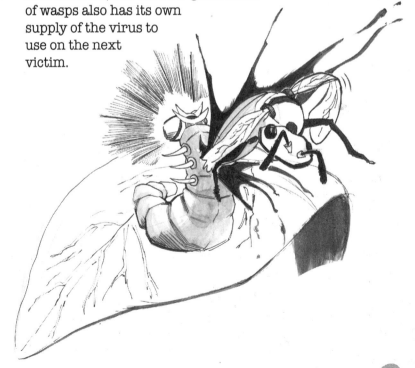

For the Birds

Not every relationship benefits everyone involved; some relationships work for one species but have no effect on the other. Remember the housekeeping army ants? In the tropics of South America, at least 50 species of birds make use of the disturbance created by marching army ants. As the ants march along, other insects attempt to escape just ahead of the infantry, scurrying and flying around in an understandable panic. These birds, most notably the ant birds (Thamnophilidae), dine out by catching insects frightened out of hiding by the ants. As long as the birds can stay clear of the ants, they can reap the benefit of distracted, easily picked-off prey. Many species of birds are happy to exploit the flushed-out insect food source, but ant birds get more than half of their meals this way. The ants receive no benefit from the relationship, but they don't suffer from it either, because most of the fleeing insects would escape from them anyway. The relationship certainly works well for the ant birds, however, which is why they've made it a lifestyle.

Bird Cleaning Stations

Some birds are known to actually lie down near ant nests or at popular ant-foraging grounds and let the ants climb onto them. This behaviour, which is called "anting," provides the birds with a thorough grooming, leaving the ants to carry off and eat any feather mites they find. This is similar to the relationship between marine fish and cleaner wrasses or cleaner shrimp, which groom para-sites off client fish at popular cleaning stations.

Social Groups, Large and Small

We humans think we're pretty sophisticated, our social structure having blossomed from small family units and then villages to huge urban centres and decentralized governments. We were not actually the first to form societies; insects beat us in that race, too, by many millions of years. Many insect groups have never bothered with societies, and others have embraced sociality wholeheartedly. Societies, insect or otherwise, have arisen from increasingly complex strategies of parental care. Parenting for most arthropods consists of little more than choosing a healthy mate and an appropriate time or place to lay eggs. Under certain conditions, however, more offspring will survive if a parent is around to defend them when they are most vulnerable.

Single Insect Dads

The eggs of the Southwestern giant water bug (Hemiptera: Belostomatidae: *Abedus indentatus*) can only hatch successfully if they are tended to constantly, cleaned of fungus, protected from hungry snails, kept warm and exposed to fresh air now and then. The easiest way for the water bug to manage all this is to glue the eggs to the wings of a parent—in this species, the male. Single Dads are nowhere near as common as single Mums in the insect world, but they do exist. For the Southwestern giant water bug, it is better to leave the egg-sitting to the male, so the females are free to hunt prey, get fat and produce more eggs with greater yolk stores to nourish the unhatched young. Females attach their eggs, one at a time, to the wings, thorax and even head of their mate, and he keeps them warm and clear of danger—even doing push-ups at the water's surface to give them air. Once they hatch and moult, the water-bug nymphs are ready to swim and catch their own prey, and Dad is free, as the eggshells come unglued from his body.

Getting Along

Bug Parenting

Egg and hatchling guarding is especially useful when the risk of cannibalism or egg parasitism is high. If insects are feeding out in plain sight—on leaves, in the case of stink bugs (Hemiptera: Pentatomidae) and leaf beetles (Chrysomelidae)—nearby parents can provide shelter for nymphs and larvae when danger strikes. Burying beetles (Silphidae: *Nicrophorus* spp.) feed on small, dead vertebrates such as mice, which must be buried before flies, fungi and bacteria can get to them. The mother or both parents clean, bury and entomb the carcass before spraying it with antibiotic juices. When the eggs hatch, the larvae are fed regurgitated, predigested flesh from the buried carcass. Just like baby birds, the larvae rear their little heads to receive the meal from their parent's jaws. Soon, they can feed themselves but only because of the efforts the adults made to protect and preserve a short-lived food source.

Giving Family Dinners a Whole New Meaning

Wood roaches (Blattodea: Cryptocercidae) of North America, which live in extended family groups that feed and huddle together in hollow rotting logs, are considered semi-social. The roaches need their extended family members to provide a reliable supply of the protozoan organisms used to digest the decomposing wood they eat. These organisms live in the roaches' hindguts. Whenever the wood roaches (and any other insects) moult, they also shed the lining of their fore- and hindguts, along with the wood-digesting protozoa within them. To obtain the symbionts they need, newly hatched and newly moulted wood roaches feed on the frass of their family members, sometimes directly from the source. By living with their parents and siblings, no wood roach is ever far from the protozoa they need to survive.

Peasant Rations

Like human societies in medieval Europe, social Hymenoptera typically serve a single queen. Where medieval human societies and social insects differ is that peasants are allowed to reproduce—how else could the aristocracy maintain the workforce?—whereas the only member allowed to produce young in a colony of social insects is the queen. In social insect colonies, workers and soldiers are actually sterile, which means they can't bear young. How can you create a sterile workforce and ensure that only the queen can reproduce? The answer is what I call "cultivated malnutrition": the larvae destined to become workers and soldiers are fed a lower-quality diet.

Here's how it works. Honeybees (Apidae: *Apis mellifera*) actually make two kinds of honey: one is the stuff you spread on toast, the other is royal jelly, the difference being a matter of food quality. Plain old honey is just flower nectar that has been regurgitated and whisked by bee mouthparts until the water in the nectar evaporates and leaves a thick, sugary liquid. Royal jelly contains the added nutrition of pollen and vitamin B5. The sterile workforce larvae get the honey; the bee larvae destined to be queens get the royal jelly.

Bug Bite

Ants also underfeed larvae designed to become wingless adult workers and soldiers. The social bees and wasps can also reinforce their hierarchies by using sterilizing pheromones and bullying to keep the workers from breeding.

Child Labour

Termites actually use child labour in their societies. The young termites work to maintain the colony from the moment they hatch and can change later in life to become workers or soldiers. Termite royalty has special hormones and chemicals in its feces, which makes workers and soldiers sterile when they eat it. Remember that most termites need to feed on the poop from others to get the protists that help them digest wood. They have no choice but to accept these meals, even if it leaves them unable to have young of their own.

Family Ties

Human peasants sick of starvation rations have historically stormed the palace and overthrown the spoiled, greedy royalty. So why don't worker ants revolt? The insects tolerate this seemingly unfair system for good reason: family ties. Unlike human society, all the workers and soldiers in an insect colony are closely related to each other and the queen. Termites in a colony are all brothers and sisters, and the social Hymenoptera of any given colony are all sisters. In fact, the sister ants, bees and wasps in a colony are more closely related to each other than they are to their own mother, the queen. Giving up the ability to have your own children isn't so bad if it means rearing new queens and drones (males) that share 75 percent of your genes. These closely related hymenopteran sisters share only 50 percent of their genes with the queen, just as you share 50 percent of your genes with your mother, father or siblings.

We're All in This Together

The increased relatedness in the sister workers and soldiers helps the social Hymenoptera behave as one super-organism instead of millions of selfish individuals. So the reason for the bees', wasps' and ants' social success lies in their extremely tight-knit families. Perhaps this is the only way such a large group of organisms can work together toward a common goal—the goal benefits every one of them. Can you imagine living in a family of millions of siblings, and no one argues about whose turn it is to do the dishes?

Needed: One Million Babysitters

Do social insects know something we don't? There must be some advantage to working together—the sheer abundance of the truly social bees, wasps, ants and termites serves as a testament to this. There are many more species of non-social bees and wasps than there are social species, but, when it comes to individual numbers, the socialites win, hands-down. Why are there so many of them? Many more helpless larvae can be fed and raised by a dedicated team of a million ant sisters than by a single queen. The general hierarchy of insect societies is pretty harsh by modern human standards, but it has lasted longer than any human society has, so far.

The Argentine Ant Empire

One of the world's most invasive species, the Argentine ant (*Linepithema humile*), a native of South America, has spread to six other continents since the 1900s. They have succeeded because these new environments lack the predators, diseases and parasites that normally keep the ant's population in check. The Argentine ants can form supercolonies, in which many connected nests, each with multiple, related queens, work together. Unlike the native ant colonies in the areas the Argentine ant has invaded, which fight among themselves, the Argentines cooperate with each other. Just as smaller tribes and nations of humans have historically fallen to larger empires, so too have native ants in the face of the Argentine ant. One supercolony of Argentine ants stretches from Italy to Spain—at least 6000 kilometres, with millions of related, connected nests. The potential damage to the newly colonized ecosystems because of the loss of native ants is unimaginable.

Bug Bite

If all the living things in the world were piled onto a scale and weighed together, the ants would make up 15 percent of the total weight of all life on Earth!

Rules of the Road

We can learn a lot of things from the ants—how to deal with traffic jams, for example. Although the largest human cities dwarf all but the greatest ant colonies in terms of numbers, when it comes to managing traffic flow, we have similar problems. Whether it's a bottleneck at a tunnel opening or a lineup on a narrow stretch of road, clogged traffic caused by steady streams of individuals travelling in different directions is a problem that all large societies have to cope with. In human systems, drivers merging into different lanes of traffic are supposed to alternate fairly, but impatient individuals make decisions for their own benefit, sometimes to the detriment of others. Too many selfish people making moves to get around the heavy traffic usually just create the delays they're trying to avoid.

When it comes to traffic flow, ants are miles ahead of us. Scientists have performed experiments by placing narrow bridges, with enough room for only two single-file streams of ants to pass, along foraging routes. Along these high-traffic areas are "empty-handed" workers heading out for more food, weighed-down ants returning with food and scouts returning with new food-gathering sites in mind. Just like a large truck with a heavy load, ants with food travel slower than ants carrying nothing, so the ants leaving the colony and the scouts returning can move faster than the food-laden ants. In a human system, the returning faster traffic (the scouts) try to pass the slower vehicles (the food-carrying ants), resulting in head-on collisions with the outgoing flow (the empty-handed ants).

In the ant system, however, the workers carrying food take priority and are allowed to pass first. The empty-handed ants travelling in the same direction as the laden workers get to move, too, but only as fast as the slower ants. To allow each ant to cross the bridge one at a time would waste precious foraging time, so the ants let the traffic dictate which group goes first. A group of returning ants will cross the bridge in unison, then a group of outbound ants and so on.

What's interesting is that the inbound ants without food do not try to pass slower workers; instead, they patiently slow down and move as one. This is actually faster than speeding ahead and running into groups of outbound traffic over and over. By travelling as one group in the same direction, with rules determining who goes first at bottlenecks, ants waste less time in traffic jams and accidents than we do.

Of course, humans aren't serving the same queen or working toward a common goal while driving—each person is trying to get home as fast as possible, forget about everyone else. What we can learn from ants is how making decisions for the benefit of everyone could actually reduce everyone's commuting time. For one thing, they walk everywhere.

Not Getting Along

Waging War

Like humans, insects have societal practices that aren't so popular. There are unflattering similarities between social insects and humans, one of which is the practice of warfare. When a group of insects coordinate an attack on another colony to steal food, workers or territory, it can be considered war, just as it is when humans attack other countries. Really, warfare is similar to individual animals fighting for resources but involves larger numbers of individuals cooperating to either attack or defend against the other group.

Ant Attackers

Ant colonies will make organized raids on nearby nests that are competitors for the same food sources. At certain times of year, the amount of seeds, dead insects or other food matter can dwindle, causing ants to forage in new territory and sometimes in other, smaller ant colonies. Using pheromones to maintain trails and group activity, workers and soldiers will attack, kill and carry off other adult ants and steal food stores, eggs, larvae and pupae from their enemies' nests.

Horrifying Hornets

Ants are not the only social insects to practice warfare. In fact, several species of hornets are known to make organized attacks on bee colonies. Japanese giant hornets (*Vespa mandarina japonica*), which can reach a body length of more than 5 centimetres, will seek out a bee colony to steal their larvae and honey, and, when they do, an attack soon follows.

Using pheromones like chemical messages, the hornets form raiding parties of about 30 and can completely destroy a 30,000-member bee colony. Because the hornets are much larger than the bees, they are not easily warded off by the stinging defenders, and one attacking hornet can kill 40 bees per minute.

Once they have eliminated all resistance, they move in and carry off the helpless bee larvae and as much honey as they can eat, leaving a pile of legs and other severed bee parts in their wake. The bee-attacking Japanese giant hornets also catch and kill mantids, katydids and other large insect prey.

Bug Bite

Japanese giant hornets can cut a honeybee right in half with a single bite! Although their stingers are 6 millimetres long and they deliver one of the most powerful stings of any insect, the hornets don't use them on their prey. Instead, they bite.

Besieged Bees

War is not just about the attack—sometimes defense is the only means of survival. Japanese honeybees (*Apis cerana japonica*) have a clever way of defending themselves against giant hornets. When the first hornet scout arrives, it marks the beehive with pheromone and then goes back home to lead others to the nest. When the Japanese honeybees notice a hornet scout, they take immediate action by mobbing the intruder, surrounding it with hundreds of bee bodies. The bees then start to flex their wing muscles without moving their wings, which creates heat. The temperature in the ball of flexing bees increases to 46°C, enough to kill the trapped hornet but not the bees. The bees will start to die at 47°C, so they run the risk of losing a few workers, but it's worth a few losses to avoid total destruction in the jaws of the hornets. Talk about a warm welcome!

Not Getting Along

Slavery

Wasps and ants have also developed slavery. By forcing members of other colonies to work without the benefit of helping their own families, slave-making ants and wasps get extra workers, without needing to go through the trouble of raising them from eggs. Just as humans once did—and sometimes still do—insects use slaves as cheap labour and sometimes use violence and intimidation to maintain their power.

Slave Raids

Ants will return from a raid with eggs and pupae from another colony and sometimes rear them into adults, which then serve their new queen. This tends to occur when the raiding ants return with a good haul of stolen food as well as plenty of stolen young. Because they have enough food to stock the pantry, the ants don't need to devour the eggs, larvae or pupae and instead tend to them until they emerge as adults. The adult slave ants work just as hard as the colony members—but for a queen that's not their mother. Slave ants are not usually allowed to look after the young or the queen; they're assigned to nest maintenance, garbage duty and foraging for their masters.

Slave Wages

Is the life of a slave ant any worse than a "free" worker serving in its own colony? The workload is no different for a slave ant than for a "free" ant; the difference is that the slave ant is not working to raise its sisters and so receives no benefit in the form of nieces and nephews that found new colonies as males and new queens. The only reason worker ants, which are unable to have their own young, aren't at a disadvantage is that they are working to ensure that most of their own genes are passed on by their fertile siblings. A slave ant works for no benefit to itself, direct or indirect, because it knows nothing else. These ants were raised to help the colony in their own nest and just happen to have been stolen to work for another boss.

Interestingly, ant colonies that take slaves have usually lost much of their own workforce to warfare and slave-making raids by another nest. Without enough sisters to share the work of feeding the queen, tending the eggs, feeding the larvae, managing waste, repairing the tunnels, foraging and defense, the colony would collapse. The only solution is to shanghai their neighbour's young and force them to work as slaves.

Bug Bite

Ants, like some humans, are victims of a cycle of abuse: ant colonies that are victims of slave-making raids in turn steal their own slaves from another colony, and the cycle repeats. Whether ants have developed forgiveness, as select humans have, is unlikely, though some have better relationships with their neighbours than others.

Not Getting Along

Under New Management

Some species of wasps are not capable of starting their own colonies, so, instead, they simply find another species' colony and take it over. The Boreal yellowjacket (*Vespula austriaca*) is a wasp that doesn't produce workers of its own but still needs workers to rear the young, which are all fertile queens and males. It accomplishes this by finding a colony of Forest yellowjackets (*Vespula acadica*) with a queen of their own and taking control. The Boreal yellowjacket female bites and bullies the Forest yellowjacket queen and her workers, even executing a few as examples to the others. Because she needs enough workers to raise her offspring, she lets the old queen live until she stops laying eggs. The old queen is then also done away with. Now the invader has the old queen's workforce to do her bidding, and, if they don't, she bites them into submission, forcing them to regurgitate food for her. They carry on feeding the young, but the larvae are not their siblings. Commandeered by a new queen to rear larvae unrelated to them, the old workers have become slaves in their own nest!

Cannibalism

Cannibalism is the practice of eating one's own species. The word conjures up images of headhunters salivating at the sight of plump European explorers. Insects were already well versed in cannibalism before humans took to looking at their neighbours as menu items: spiders, mantids and other insects often eat their own.

Off with His Head!

Quite possibly the most famous cannibals are praying mantids (Mantodea), which are known for a tendency to devour their mates. To be fair to the mantids, much of this reputation stems from artificial laboratory conditions in which hungry females eat a less-varied diet than they would in the wild. Unfortunately, when a male comes along, it looks more like a Big Mac than Romeo.

Regardless of conditions, males are very cautious of their mates; they will retreat if a female is too aggressive and leave quickly after mating. The female isn't always keen to say goodbye, though, and will reach back and tear off the male's head—along with the brain inside it, which should have told him to look for another female. Tearing the male's head off not only provides the female with a decent meal, right when she needs to put energy into developing eggs, but it also ensures that most of her eggs are fertilized.

Bug Bite

The hungrier a female mantid is, the more likely she is to eat her mate. Also, a hungry female that ate the male will have healthier offspring than one that didn't. The better-fed the mother is, the healthier her young will be. If the male mantids knew this, they might consider serving dinner *before* mating.

Dinner First

Many spiders, such as the famous Black widows (Theridiidae: *Latrodectus* sp.), practice copulatory cannibalism (the act of eating one's mate), and the most reasonable explanation for it is called the "spillover" hypothesis. Essentially, for a female spider to grow up healthy, she has to be aggressive and respond quickly to prey. These killer instincts keep her fed and allow her to grow into an adult. Her tendency to eat the male, sometimes before they even mate, is thought to be a "spillover" of this aggressive tactic. It takes a while for the concept of suitor to sink in, and the first few dates never get past dinner.

Not Even a Good Snack

Unlike the mantids, most male spiders are much smaller than their female counterparts and wouldn't make a satisfying meal. Why are they so small? It's believed that, initially, there were many different sizes of male spiders. Unfortunately, the large ones, which made a better meal than the smaller ones, were eaten before they got a chance to pass on their "large male" genes. Only the tiniest males, too small to trigger a predatory response in the female, managed to father offspring, resulting in tiny males and large females. Another explanation is that natural selection favoured bigger females, which could put on enough fat to supply their eggs with rich yolk, resulting in better-fed spiderlings. This would make the small males seem even smaller.

The Need to Feed

Cockroaches are also cannibals—just when you thought they couldn't get any worse. Although eating your own kind is hardly endearing, sometimes, in insect circles, at least, the circumstances call for it. Cockroaches are generalist omnivores, which means they are happy to eat almost anything, including dead insects. If their diet is poor in protein, they find creative ways of putting meat on the menu. Normally peaceful roaches will devour their brothers and sisters when they are moulting, or immediately after, while the exoskeletons are still soft. Feed the roaches dog food, however, and the incidence of cannibalism drops immediately.

Protein Supplement

More than 300 million years of cockroach history tells us that the practice of cannibalism arises to meet specific dietary demands. Interestingly, the same is true of humans. Historically, human cannibals lived in places unable to support domestic livestock; they had to hunt for meat. When the environment of a local society—the crops and other food supplies—doesn't provide all the nutritional requirements of the people, humans become a protein supplement.

Cannibalism has also occurred in North American Native groups but not as an accepted practice. Sometimes, a sort of cabin fever, or "bush madness," strikes starved individuals mid-winter, causing them to try to eat their families. According to Native folklore, people struck by this urge are possessed by a giant hairy forest spirit, known to Western Cree as the *Wetigo*. Whether or not this is the greatest trick ever played on humans by Sasquatch is yet to be determined.

Bad News Bugs

Fleas

Humans have struggled with our insect contemporaries since we lived in caves with various external parasites (ectoparasites). Fleas and bedbugs have waited for us in our beds for probably two million years, and it's possible that our modern intolerance of them indoors is an inherited trait. Fleas (Siphonaptera) deserve recognition beyond their abilities as high jumpers, notably for spending 150 million years perfecting the fine art of stealing mammal blood.

Bug Bite

When it comes to bloodsucking, fleas make life easy for themselves. They hang out in our own homes, sometimes living right on the host, like the fleas that plague cats and dogs. Their larvae are caterpillar-like and crawl around the nests of the host, feeding on the excrement of the adults and preying on other small invertebrates and each other.

Bugs with Bite

Fleas are largely responsible for many pandemics (worldwide outbreaks) of plague that have taken heavy tolls on human populations through time. Carried by rats, most notably the Black and Norwegian rats (*Rattus rattus*,

R. norvegicus, respectively), Oriental rat fleas (*Xenopsylla cheopis*) hosting plague bacteria (*Yersinia pestis*) have bitten their way into history.

Plagued by Fleas

How do fleas transmit the plague? The flea ingests plague bacteria with blood it sucks from the rat host. In the flea's digestive system, the bacteria multiply to the point where they actually block the flow of food through the gut. Because its meals aren't reaching its stomach, the infected flea gets hungry and begins to bite any host, rat or human. When a flea with a crop (an insect gizzard that helps break up food) full of bacteria tries to bite, it sucks up some blood, but because it can't swallow effectively, it regurgitates blood, and plague bacteria along with it, into the feeding site.

When the bacteria get into you, a number of things can happen: your lymph nodes can become packed with them (bubonic plague); your capillaries become blocked by them, causing blood to leak out and turn the skin black (septicemic plague); or your lungs can be infected (pneumonic plague). Once pneumonic plague develops, you have three days to live. Nasty stuff, to be sure, but the historical significance of so many human deaths cannot be overstated. Plague has been an important and recurring means of population control among humans over time. When the density of hosts (fleas, rats, people) becomes too great, disease can spread like wildfire. Fortunately, the Black Death that killed so many of our ancestors can be treated with antibiotics.

Out of Egypt

Some evidence suggests that the Nile rat (*Arvicanthis niloticus*) was a carrier of plague in ancient Egypt, and that the disease spread around the world with the arrival of the Black rat from India or Mesopotamia. When the Black rat arrived, it became a new host for the flea—and a new transportation system for spreading the plague bacteria. Black rats were also called Ship rats because of their tendency to stow away on boats, which helped them and the plague-spreading fleas move around the world.

Bug Bite

Written history has included a number of references to insect pests, including the Pharaoh's plague of locusts from Exodus and the classical Greek commentaries on flies, lice and bedbugs by Homer (800 BC), Aristotle (300 BC) and Pliny (first century AD). Although they were clearly considered enough of a nuisance to be worthy of recording, insects didn't really become the pests we consider them today until the late 1800s, when we discovered that bloodsucking insects transmitted diseases.

A Plague of Plagues

An outbreak known as Justinian's Plague occurred in 541 and killed more than 40 million people in Africa and the Mediterranean. The Black Plague spread along trade routes from Asia to Europe in the 1300s, killing 25 million people in Europe in only five years. It persisted for another 200 years in Europe. More recently, a global pandemic began in the late 1800s and carried on to 1948, killing 12 million people in India alone. This outbreak also managed to reach North and South America, with most cases occurring in Peru and the United States.

Some things have changed a little since Black and Norwegian rats originally brought the plague to town. It's possible that, in regions where plague still occurs, native rodents carry the bacteria, even if there are no Black or Norwegian rats around. Similarly, the Human flea (Pulicidae: *Pulex irritans*) can serve as an alternate host when the Oriental rat flea isn't around.

Mosquitoes

Mosquitoes (Diptera: Culicidae) are probably people's least favourite insect (next to cockroaches), and with good reason—adult female mosquitoes need to drink blood to produce eggs. Although you might not need every drop of blood in your body to survive, no one likes to donate it to the mosquitoes. Mosquitoes also spread diseases; when they feed, they can easily pick up parasites from one host and then infect the next when they feed again.

Bug Bite

Unlike female mosquitoes, male mosquitoes don't drink blood; they drink plant juices and nectar but never bite animals.

Pestilent Pests

Mosquitoes are the single most significant group of arthropods affecting human health. They can spread many different harmful organisms, including protozoa (kingdom Protista) that cause malaria; nematode worms (kingdom Animalia: phylum Nematoda) that cause disfiguration as they chew through your body; and no less than 250 different viruses. Luckily, they do not spread very many kinds of bacteria (kingdom Bacteria), though they can transmit anthrax if they bite an infected mammal first.

Anthrax (*Bacillus anthracis*) is a bacterium found in areas where humans raise livestock such as cows, goats or sheep. Eating, inhaling or getting anthrax under your skin can be deadly. If a mosquito bites a goat that has ingested or inhaled anthrax bacteria, it can spread the disease when it bites another animal. If mosquitoes or other flies happen to land on a patch of the bacteria, they can carry the spores that get stuck to the outside of their bodies to new areas.

Malarial Mosquitoes

Malaria is a disease caused by protozoa (*Plasmodium* sp., most serious is *P. falciparum*) that multiply inside your blood cells and liver. Every year, 1.5 to 2.8 million people die from malaria worldwide. Most of them are young children in Africa, south of the Sahara Desert. The disease is spread by several species of mosquitoes, which ingest the parasite when they bite an infected human and drink the blood. Inside the mosquito, the malaria reproduces and finds its way to the saliva glands. When the mosquito bites its next victim, the malaria is injected into the next human host. According to some sources, 1.6 billion people worldwide are directly at risk of malaria infection from mosquito bites, which is almost one in four.

Nasty But Important

So, why do we have mosquitoes, anyway? It's difficult to see the usefulness of a group of annoying blood feeders. But mosquitoes, like many other annoying insects, play an important part in the environment. As larvae, they feed on particles in the water or other small animals, including other mosquito larvae. They are, in turn, eaten by larger aquatic insects, fish, spiders and amphibians.

As adults, they drink from flowers, aiding in pollination, and they serve as food for spiders, dragonflies, bats and birds, to name a few. If you consider their universality as a meal in the food web and their role as disease carrier—the lowly mosquito could be responsible for no less than 1.5 million human deaths per year—it becomes obvious just how significant they are.

Why is spreading disease significant? Just like every other living thing in the web of life, humans also need our population controlled—and it is—by natural disasters and diseases. Sounds harsh, but the cold, hard fact is that, if we let our population grow unchecked, we'd be forced to fight each other for food and space, we'd starve to death and we'd probably push many other Earthlings to extinction, as well. Remember the aphids, with their possible 6 billion offspring from a single mother in a single year? If they weren't being eaten by predators and parasitoids and killed by diseases, the world would be overrun by aphids, which would eat every plant on the planet.

Could Be Worse

Be glad you don't live in Rangoon, Myanmar, where the population can receive 80,000 mosquito bites per person, per year. In Northern Canada, the Snow pool mosquito (*Ochlerotatus* sp.) emerges in huge numbers every spring and can bite exposed skin at a rate of 280 to 300 bites per minute. At that rate, you could lose half of your blood in 90 minutes, so I wouldn't advise sleeping outside under the stars. I wouldn't hold it against the people of Rangoon or our Canadian territories were they to have a low opinion of mosquitoes. The rest of us should remember how lucky we are to only consider them a minor annoyance and not a significant source of blood loss or a fatal disease carrier.

Bug Bite

If you would like to turn
the tables and annoy the
mosquitoes for a change,
contribute to Spreadthenet.org, a worldwide organization
that supplies mosquito nets to malaria-stricken areas.
You could help make a serious dent in the number
of people who die every year from malaria
and countless other preventable
mosquito-borne illnesses.

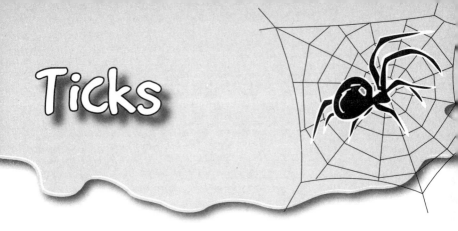

Ticks

Ticks (Ixodida) are arachnids, like spiders and scorpions, though they are more closely related to mites. As young, they only have six legs but develop the full arachnid complement of eight legs as adults. All ticks feed on vertebrates, especially birds and mammals. Ticks feed on blood throughout their lives, and both males and females need blood to survive.

Questing for Blood

Many ticks feed on one or a few different animal hosts, but first they need to locate one, which they do by looking for places where they might run into their desired host. This can mean waiting in the animal's nest or burrow, or along a trail that the animal uses, until it shows up. Ticks will climb up a blade of grass or other plant to reach the shoulder height of their preferred animal host. So, if a tick is hoping to hop onto a moose, it needs to climb higher than a tick looking for a rabbit. Ticks are also very sensitive to the smell of carbon dioxide and other gases exhaled or eliminated by animals. Some ticks, in their quest for a host, even run toward any moving object that is the right size.

Parasi-tick

Ticks have become entirely parasitic, which means all members of the group eat nothing but blood. Like spiders, they can only ingest liquids, and blood is a very nutritious liquid, indeed. Their mouthparts work like little cutting knives to break through the skin of the host and also serve to anchor the tick in place while it feeds. The curved spines on their mouthparts and a glue-like substance they produce are what make ticks so difficult to remove. Ticks usually only hang around long enough to get full—but this can take days or even weeks. Ticks can gain enough energy and sustenance from one meal to manage a moult to the next size.

Spreading Lyme

As blood feeders, ticks carry many serious diseases that affect livestock, wildlife and humans around the world. Although mosquitoes spread diseases that affect more people than any other arthropod, ticks can spread a wider variety of harmful organisms, including Lyme disease, relapsing fever, Rocky Mountain spotted fever, tularemia and anaplasmosis. Lyme disease is caused by a few species of *Borrelia* bacteria, which people get from being bitten by infected species of *Ixodes* ticks, such as the Western Black-legged tick (*I. pacificus*). The symptoms usually start as a circular "bull's eye" rash around the bite and can develop over time to include fever, stiff joints and, left untreated, even paralysis.

Fortunately, most of the disease spreading doesn't occur until the tick has fed for more than 24 hours. By checking yourself thoroughly after spending time in wild areas, especially those with long grass, you might be able to remove the tick before catching anything serious. If you can avoid being bitten altogether, that's even better. By wearing DEET bug spray and long sleeves and pants when venturing into the woods or camping, you can probably avoid most incidents. If you are bitten, carefully remove the tick and its mouthparts and clean the bite well. Keep an eye out for rashes, and see a doctor if you don't feel well. Antibiotics given early on will treat almost anything you can get from a tick.

Bug Bite

Although most ticks only spend long enough on their hosts to get one meal of blood, that can be one seriously large meal. Ticks, especially adult females, can gorge themselves to the point where they increase 200 to 600 times their original weight. That would be like you going for lunch and coming back weighing as much as an African elephant!

Other Bloodsuckers

Why do some insects and arachnids suck blood? Because blood is a high-quality food. It is easy to digest and is chock-full of nutrients that are being carried to our cells and organs. If you can steal some, it's a good meal. Just don't get caught in the act.

Painkillers

Most bloodsuckers have clever ways of not being detected by the understandably upset host. Perhaps the most common tactic is to produce some sort of anesthetic, a painkiller, which is injected as the animal feeds. Anesthetic is used by mosquitoes, ticks (Acari: Ixodida), fleas (Siphonaptera), bedbugs (Hemiptera: Cimicidae) and kissing bugs (Hemiptera: Reduviidae), to name a few. Even Vampire bats (*Desmodus rotundus*) have anesthetic saliva!

Sneaking a Snack

Bloodsucking is a risky business, so bloodsuckers need to be cautious. Most blood-feeding animals try to approach sleeping hosts, stepping very lightly, and will retreat at the slightest sign of movement. Those that steal blood in broad daylight must be quick about it or choose an area that isn't easy to swat, such as when a mosquito lands on your back, for example, and bites you through your T-shirt. Ticks employ another strategy: cementing themselves into place for as long as it takes to feed. They, too, choose hard-to-reach places, such as behind the ears, and they glue their own mouthparts in, making it hard to remove them, even if they're discovered.

Becoming a Vampire

The Reduviid family includes predatory species, such as assassin bugs, and parasitic blood feeders, such as kissing bugs. Assassin bugs use piercing mouthparts to inject digestive juices and suck out the insides of insects, which are killed in the process. Kissing bugs feed only on the blood of larger animals. Their feeding method is the same as the assassin's, however: stab, inject fluid and suck, which suggests that they might have been more like assassins bugs in the distant past. Because a large animal can provide multiple meals, it makes sense that the kissing bugs made the switch.

Bug Bite

Kissing bugs can go nine months between meals without starving to death. Some tarantulas have gone more than two years without eating. Humans can manage about 45 days. The major difference in how long we can survive without food has to do with how quickly we burn energy. Insects and arachnids, like reptiles, can reduce their energy demands by cooling down and being inactive when there's little to eat. Humans and other mammals, however, burn energy like living SUVs, using up most of the fuel we get from food just to keep our bodies at a constant 37°C.

Kissing Bug 1, Darwin 0

Charles Darwin found Triatomines, the bloodsucking subfamily that includes the kissing bug (*Rhodnius prolixus*), so interesting that he brought one home from South America to show his colleagues. He allowed himself to be bitten as a demonstration of the insect's adaptations and very likely contracted a protozoan blood parasite (*Trypanosoma cruzi*) that wasn't formally described until the early 20th century. What he had was probably Chagas' disease, which causes as many as 50,000 deaths and affects tens of millions of people every year in South and Central America. Darwin suffered poor health and exhaustion for the rest of his life.

People Drink Blood, Too

Should the thought of drinking blood seem like something only zombies and vampires would do, consider the Masai people of Kenya. They might possibly be the only humans to have added hematophagy (eating blood) to their pastoral lifestyle. The Masai raise cattle, drink milk and eat beef like most people, but they also bleed small amounts of blood from their cows. The blood is mixed with milk for a nutritious meal. Although some might consider this practice parasitic, it really isn't—the Masai take good care of their cows, making the relationship more mutual, or cooperative, than exploitative.

Meat Eaters

Although mosquitoes, fleas and black flies do bite people, they don't spend much time in contact with their hosts. Other groups, though, have evolved to exploit the nutritious food source that is living tissue. These groups will hang around in a host for as long as it takes to develop to their next life stage, and that might be days to months.

Living Meal

When fly larvae, also known as maggots, invade the living tissue of a vertebrate, it is called myiasis. Some flies only infect an open wound if the opportunity presents itself (facultative myiasis) and otherwise grow up by eating the tissues of dead animals. Others are capable of burrowing into healthy flesh, and many can only survive by living inside a living host as larvae (obligate myiasis). Flies that only go for living tissue when they get a chance are less of a nuisance than those that have no choice but to use you as a living bed and breakfast.

Maggot Medics

Even regular old Blue bottle flies (Calliphoridae: *Calliphora vomitoria*) can get into a wound and feed on the dead and dying tissue. Although the idea seems pretty disgusting, having flies dine on dead tissue can actually help a person with a festering injury. First observed in field hospitals, where conditions allowed flies to reach bedridden soldiers, small numbers of fly larvae (maggots) can help remove dead tissue; they also provide antibiotic chemicals that slow the rate of decomposition—the result is a cleaner wound. More is not always better, though: too many maggots in a wound can actually hasten a patient's demise, leaving the flies with plenty of carrion for later.

Bug Bite

For much of human history, war has provided parasitic insects with an abundance of hosts crowded into confined spaces. Until World War II, when better hospital conditions, medicine and delousing procedures were introduced, the Human body louse (Phthiraptera: Pediculidae: *Pediculus humanus corporis*) killed more soldiers than ever died in battle. The lice spread diseases, such as epidemic typhus and relapsing fever, among the bedridden patients in field hospitals and soldiers in crowded trenches.

Botflies

Oestridae, known as botflies, is a family of flies that make Blue bottles seem polite by comparison. Botflies are all parasites and must invade a living host in which to mature. Their larvae are plump and have stiff spike-like setae (bug hairs) that prevent their removal until they are ready to pupate. The botflies usually prefer one kind of animal to use as a host, though they can potentially survive in any one of a few different species and are well adapted to do so.

Adults do not feed, and some do not develop mouthparts at all. With the exception of the Human botfly (*Dermatobia hominis*), the larvae in this family typically migrate from the site of entry to the muscles, tongue or stomach, for example, where development takes place. Some are ingested as eggs cleverly attached to the host's favourite food plant, others actively climb into the nose or mouth and still others are airlifted by their mother and dropped into the nose or mouth.

Human Botflies

The female Human botfly catches mosquitoes and black flies in midair and glues up to 30 of her eggs to them. When the smaller flies land on a human to bite, the botfly eggs sense the heat of the body and drop off to hatch on the host. Most botfly larvae burrow in, feed and grow in the mouth or sinuses and then migrate under the skin of the host, where they complete their development. The Human botfly stays in the same place throughout larval growth and becomes disturbingly large, feeding on blood and tissue and breathing through an opening to the surface. Should you ever find yourself a host for the Human botfly, perhaps after a jaunt to Central America, you can defeat the parasite by covering the opening with petroleum jelly. After a day or two, the larva will have suffocated and can be pulled out. One of the nastiest things I have witnessed was the removal of a bulbous botfly larva from a woman's scalp, leaving a hole as thick as a pencil.

Mites on Your Face

More than 90 percent of us have Human follicle mites (Prostigmata: Demodicidae: *Demodex folliculorum hominis* and *D. brevis*) living on the skin of our eyebrows, forehead and nose. These mites wriggle into the follicle at the base of the hairs on the face and either feed there or inside the sebaceous gland that secretes oil to keep our skin soft. From here, they use their needle-like mouthparts to pierce the living skin cells and suck their juices. Although most people are not affected by their follicle mites, some can develop rashes and other skin problems.

Hitchhikers

Many insects and arachnids spend time on their host without causing serious damage—or any damage at all. Sometimes, free-living mites hitch a ride on a beetle or millipede, which carries them to a new food source, and they hop off once they arrive. This hitchhiking is called phoresy, and it's an excellent way to travel long distances if you don't have wings. Some phoresy lasts just long enough to get off at the next stop; in other cases, it can last for the life of the hitchhiker. Several families of avian nasal mites, which live in the nostrils of birds, feed on the skin inside the sinuses, making them parasites, but some species are not harmful. Some of the nasal mites that live on hummingbirds run out of the nostrils and down the beak to feed on nectar as the bird visits flowers.

Copycats, Show-offs and Disguises

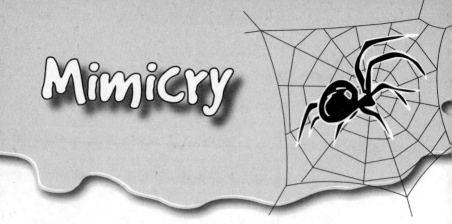

Mimicry

Mimicry is when organisms have come to resemble each other, using the same colours or patterns, for example, to protect themselves from enemies. Sometimes insects and other animals look alike because they're sending out similar messages. Sometimes the messages are true, but sometimes they're not.

Copycats

Some unrelated species send out the same type of message but for different reasons. When species look similar because they are all poisonous, they are using the same true signals that tell a predator to leave them alone (Mullerian mimicry). When

species that are not poisonous or dangerous resemble those that are, the copycat insect gains protection by tricking predators into thinking it's toxic, when it isn't (Batesian mimicry).

Copycats, Show-offs and Disguises

Will the Real Monarch Please Stand Up?

In North America, there are two species of butterflies with similar colouring: the Monarch butterfly (*Danaus plexippus*) and the Viceroy (*Limenitis archippus*). The Monarch is toxic—it becomes toxic by feeding on milkweed as caterpillars. The toxins that the plant produces to defend itself from insect predators have no effect on the Monarch larvae, and they store the toxins to use for their own defense. (When a substance is obtained through the diet and co-opted for another use, it's called sequestration.) The Monarchs are brightly coloured: the caterpillars are striped in yellow, black and white, and the adults are orange, black and white. This colouration, which is obvious and easy to remember, warns predators that the Monarch is unpleasant to eat. Scientists call this kind of advertisement aposematic colouration.

Experiments have shown that birds don't learn to avoid Monarchs until they taste one for themselves. Finding it to be disgusting, birds learn that orange, black and white butterflies aren't good eating. For years, it was believed that the Viceroy, which looks almost identical to the Monarch, was a copycat and a cheat, with no toxins of its own. But here's the odd thing: the Viceroy could only manage as a cheat if birds had already learned to avoid the Monarch, which means that, without the Monarch, the mimic would be defenseless. Apparently, no one ever bothered to taste a Viceroy, because it turns out that they are toxic, too. Both species are toxic and use the same, honest colour signals to avoid being eaten. So the Monarch and Viceroy are both toxic examples of Mullerian mimicry, and don't let anyone tell you otherwise.

Stingers and Cheaters

Many of us have learned to avoid black-and-yellow buzz-ing insects, thanks to previous experiences with bees and wasps, usually in childhood. The bright, contrasting colours that many of the social Hymenoptera wear are there to warn would-be predators of their painful stings. These stinging black-and-yellow insects are members of a mimicry complex, in which the warning is valid, and many equally toxic groups use the same basic signals.

But, there are cheats, too. Hoverflies (Diptera: Syrphidae), bee flies (Bombyliidae) and bee-mimicking scarab beetles (*Trichiotinus* sp.) take advantage of the well-known association between black-and-yellow stripes and insects that are best avoided. Hoverflies, for example, look just like a housefly with a black-and-yellow paint-job. These cheats only benefit from wearing team colours, however, if the real stingers (the bees and wasps) are present in equal or greater numbers. In human terms, the hoverflies are like wimps who wear ninja costumes; because they look like they have martial arts training, you're not likely to pick a fight with them.

Copycats, Show-offs and Disguises

Bug Bite

When it comes to mimicry, there are always more honest signallers than cheats. This is because a predator only learns to avoid the bright-coloured species after it eats one and gets sick or stung. If too many phonies were out there, the predators would learn that not all brightly coloured prey are nasty, and the cheats would lose their advantage. Take my advice: if it looks like a wasp, don't mess with it, and if it's so colourful that it stands out, don't touch it.

Now You See Me

Some insects and spiders sport bright colours for other reasons than to advertise their toxic or dangerous status. The bright colours and patterns can help identify the opposite sex or tell something about the quality of a potential mate. Sometimes, the colours can send several signals at once.

Butterfly Ballet

Although male and female Morpho butterflies (Nymphalidae: *Morpho* spp.) of South and Central America are well camouflaged on the undersides of their wings, the upper sides are a beautiful iridescent blue. Males have more blue on the upper sides of their wings than the females and use their half-coloured, half-camouflaged pattern to their advantage. Males have ritualized flight patterns—much like a flying dance they perform to show off to a female. Females are watching to see the flashes of blue upper wings take place at the right point in the dance, evidence that the displaying male is a strong flier. She can also tell that he must have been well fed as a larva to develop such nice wing colour and has managed to avoid predators that would have damaged his wings. All these pluses make him a good choice as a mate.

Flashy Flappers

Morphos make difficult prey for birds, because the birds
see different colours when the butterfly is in flight. The
bright blue upper sides periodically catch the sunlight in
a burst of colour and then are hidden, as the wings flap
again. If the Morpho was dull and camouflaged, without
the blinding flashes of shiny blue, it might be easier to
follow. To make things even more difficult for predators,
male Morphos fly unpredictably, often gaining height,
flashing blue at the peak of their climb and then diving
with the blue hidden by the dull underside of the wings.

Spider Show-offs

Jumping spiders also use bright colours to advertise
more than danger. Family Salticidae is probably the
largest family of spiders, with 5000 species worldwide.

Unlike most spiders, jumpers can see quite well, an adaptation that helps with their jumping lifestyle. Being able to see where you're about to leap is useful for catching prey, but jumpers also need to see each other. With this family's good vision comes a whole world of visual signals the spiders use to communicate with each other. Males and females of some species of jumping spiders look so different that they have been incorrectly identified as different species. We see very brightly coloured males, often with tufts of hairs and contrasting patterns, that wave their legs and those little limbs on either side of the fangs called palps in such a way that the larger, more conservative-looking females recognize them immediately. Here, the bright colours serve simultaneously as a warning to predators that jumpers have a nasty bite and as proof of species membership for the picky females.

Deadly Dance Partner

The Fringed jumping spider (*Portia fibriata*) from Australia can see a few centimetres farther than other species of jumpers. This allows it to see and respond to the arm-waving of approaching males belonging to different species, just as a receptive female would. When the duped males get close enough, *Portia* leaps into action, killing and eating them before they realize their mistake. Fringed jumping spiders observe and mimic the courtship of different jumpers; they use the same approach as males of the target species, to coax females out into the open and then devour them too.

Sinister Solicitor

Fringed jumping spiders show a remarkable ability to learn and problem solve. They will boldly approach the webs of other spiders, such as orb-weavers (Araneidae), and pluck the strands of silk, to mimic a struggling fly.

Copycats, Show-offs and Disguises

The other spider might respond immediately—rushing over to investigate, only to become prey itself—or it might not respond at all, in which case *Portia* will keep trying until the plucking works. If even this strategy fails, it will find another, such as rappelling from above and pulling the spider off its web by force.

Flashy Fireflies

Fireflies, which are actually beetles in the family Lampyridae, can produce flashes of light from the end of their abdomens. The ability to produce this light serves as a way for fireflies to identify their own species and the opposite sex. The distinction is also reinforced by different species flashing at different times of night, in different patterns and in different seasons. Because many different firefly species can occupy the same general habitat, they need to be able to tell each other apart. Usually males fly and flash, while females sit and watch, flashing their approval to the males with the right stuff. Males are always watching to see if they have any admirers and quickly land to mate with any that flash an invitation. After mating, the females show little interest in finding more mates, preferring to concentrate on producing eggs.

Murderous Mimics

Some species of fireflies produce toxins that make them distasteful to predators. Others do not and must acquire toxins from their diet. This has led to some pretty remarkable strategies for getting the toxins from other members of the same family. After mating, larger species in the genus *Photuris* will switch strategies and begin to respond to flashes from males of the smaller species in the genus *Photinus*. The small *Photinus* males are lured by the female *Photuris* pretending to be females of the smaller species and are eaten when they land. Why do Photinus fireflies cannibalize their *Photinus* relatives? Because *Photuris* cannot produce protective chemicals from scratch and must eat other fireflies, such as *Photinus*, to get them.

It's been shown that female *Photuris* species have learned several different flash patterns that correspond to different species, such as those in the genus *Photinus*. Male *Photuris* also flash like other species, but it's not known why. They are probably cruising for their own females, which are pretending to be smaller species so they can lure in unsuspecting chumps. If a male *Photuris* flashes

like a delicious *Photinus*, he might be invited down by a female of his own species and get a last chance to mate before being devoured.

Copycats, Show-offs and Disguises

Bug Bite

The light produced by fireflies and lightning bugs is caused by the reaction of two chemicals they produce: luciferin and luciferase. When the chemicals react, they produce light but no heat. Scientists are interested in this cold light, because they think it might be useful in helping us find a greener source of light. Much of the electrical energy running through most light bulbs (even compact fluorescents) is wasted as heat. If less energy were lost as heat, the light bulbs would be more efficient and less electricity would be needed to run them. Unfortunately, the cold light produced by the Lampyrids does give off carbon dioxide (a greenhouse gas) as a waste product, so ultimately it's not a more environmentally friendly light source.

Now You Don't

Camouflage is the shape, pattern, texture and colour used by an animal to resemble the background and make it hard to see. There is a difference between mimicry and camouflage. Mimicry uses shared or stolen signals that are usually obvious; camouflage, or crypsis, uses disguise and subtlety. Insects can demonstrate remarkable camouflage, often among groups that spend plenty of time in one spot or out in the open. Some insects even use mimicry early in life and then switch to camouflage as they age.

Pretty Predators

Mantids (Mantodea), which can look like living or dead leaves, flowers and even moss and lichen, are probably the best-known insects to use camouflage, along with the stick insects. The mantids' camouflage serves two purposes: to prevent their insect prey from noticing them until it is too late and to prevent being noticed by their own predators.

Orchid mantids (*Hymenopus coronatus*), from the jungles of Indonesia and Malaysia, look like ants when they first hatch. This keeps them safe, because most animals know better than to start a fight with anything that can call half a million sisters in for back-up. After they moult a second time, the mantids take on a pink or purple hue—which helps them do a perfect impression of the orchid buds in which they hide. As the mantids mature, they match the colours of the orchids, right down to the brown and wilted-looking adult female's wing tips, which look just like the flower petals in late season. This is an example of an insect that trades mimicry for camouflage as it gets older.

Hiding in Plain Sight

Possibly the most convincing examples of crypsis can be found in the stick and leaf insects (Phasmatodea: Phasmatidae and Phylliidae). All members of this order are incredible stick and leaf impersonators. Most are long and thin, with a texture and pattern on the exoskeleton to match their host plants. These insects tend to be slow-moving and eat an enormous number of leaves. Camouflage is useful when your lifestyle involves hanging around in trees and eating leaves—you can hide right out in the open.

Seed Mimic Eggs

The Macleay's specter stick (*Extatosoma tiaratum*), from Australia and New Guinea, has incorporated some mimicry into its camouflaged lifestyle. The adults and older nymphs resemble thorny, curled leaves, but their eggs are seed mimics. The eggs look like seeds and even have a structure on the outside that mimics an eliasome, a delicious and nutritious cap that's found on the seeds of some plants. Ants find the stick insect's eggs as they forage for seeds on the forest floor. They carry them off and consume the eliasome-like snack, leaving the eggs in the colony's larder for later. Here, in the safety of the ant nest, the stick insects inside the eggs develop and presumably absorb the odour of the colony. The ants do not seem to eat the insect eggs; because they prefer plant seeds, they eat the real ones first.

Eventually the eggs hatch, and out walk little Macleay's specters with ant-like coloration and body posture, complete with their skinny abdomens curled to look like round ant abdomens. Any other insect would be attacked if it appeared in the middle of the nest, but somehow the little stick insects pass for members of the colony long enough to walk out the nearest exit. Looking like ants also helps them move across the forest floor and up into the trees without being bothered by predators. If you look like an ant, you get treated like an ant. So the Macleay's specter stick survives as a seed mimic and an ant mimic and does quite a convincing impression of a leaf.

People and Pests

Creating Pests

With the rise of agriculture some 10,000 to 15,000 years ago, the conflict between humans and insects developed beyond parasitism and disease. As we began to dominate the landscape and alter the number and kind of species found in a given environment, we inadvertently created systems vulnerable to certain insects, and they became pests. Pests are really any life-form that does extremely well in a given habitat, so well that they dominate the community and cause damage to our crops, profits and well-being.

Variety Is the Necessity of Life

In a natural habitat, the local community is made up of many species of plants, fungi and animals. Each plant has its associated insect herbivores and the predators and parasitoids that target these insects. An aphid or caterpillar might eat a plant in its natural environment, but the plant is also protected by the feeding behaviour of predators, such as ladybugs (Coleoptera: Coccinelidae) or wasps. By attacking the plant-eating insects, the predators reduce the number of mouths that would otherwise gobble up the plants and reduce damage to the plants.

By tearing up mixed grasslands and forests and replacing them with single crops, such as wheat or lodge pole pine, we create a simplified and ultimately fragile system.

Fewer crop types attract fewer predators to keep potential pests in check, and, with too much of the same crop, any species that eats wheat or pine, for example, could become so numerous that it would be a pest. What we lose when we plant single crops is biodiversity—the variety of organisms found in an area or environment. Biodiversity lends stability to an ecosystem. In a biologically diverse environment, many different organisms perform the same job: when one species doesn't show up for work, because they all died off, many others can cover for them. If a hundred species of aphid predators live in a forest, for example, it's not a catastrophe if one species of ladybug or lacewing dies. If only one species of aphid predator existed, it would be sorely missed if it died out, and the aphids would pile up, becoming pests.

When we plant a vast area with nothing but wheat, we are planting a single species that is susceptible to the same pests, the same diseases and the same changes in conditions. Because these simple systems support fewer predators and parasitoids, pest species are allowed to run amok.

Forest Pest

In a forest, planted trees of the same species and age are vulnerable to attack at the same time. An example of how these trees can be vulnerable has to do with the Mountain pine beetle (*Dendroctonus ponderosae*) in North America. These beetles prefer older trees and act as a major control mechanism in the absence of forest fires. By attacking and killing off the older trees, the beetles make room for younger trees to grow, helping to renew the forest. By actively preventing forest fires for the past 50 years, we have unwittingly created a feast of old trees for the Mountain pine beetle. Now our concerns are focused on the loss of marketable wood, and, because there are hundreds of hectares of standing dead trees, forest fires are making a serious comeback.

What can we learn from this modern disaster? That the beetles and fires have regulated the forests for millennia, and we humans simply failed to recognize this. We thought we could save the vast majority of our forests for our own use. Our challenge now is to address the Mountain pine beetle outbreak and shift to replanting techniques that won't offer up another smorgasbord in 80 to 125 years. Other species of beetles that attack different species and ages of trees might be the next big problem for the forestry industry. Planting many different species and ages of trees and allowing more controlled burns in our forests could prevent this problem from happening again.

The Resistance

Perhaps the most important traits contributing to the success of the insects are their short generation time and large populations. Within a single human generation, hundreds of insect generations have come and gone, each complete with natural selection favouring those that adapted the best to the current conditions. Their short lives and numerous offspring allow them to respond quickly to changes in the environment. This is why, in our quest to eliminate pests, the insecticides that we develop only work for a short time; in those few years, the pests that managed to resist the insecticide have sired the next generation of resistant individuals. By trying to eliminate populations of insects, we create new populations that are invulnerable to our attacks.

Creating Resisters

In any insect population are individuals that are resistant to a given insecticide, which is why the substances and organisms we use for pest control can be more effective on some individuals than on others. For an insecticide to be ineffective, an insect only has to have slightly differently shaped receptor proteins on the surface of its nerve cells or gut lining than other members of the population. This gives the insects with those differences a potential advantage over other members of the species when we do use insecticides, leading to their success in the next generations. It also serves to reinforce how important variety is, whether it is the different kinds of life in an area or the variation among members of the same species.

Collateral Damage

The chemicals most often used to kill pests are indiscriminate, which means they kill all insects, good and bad. In fact, they can kill more beneficial insects and spiders than the pests they target. By killing predators and parasites that normally keep pest insect populations in check, we create a system prone to insect outbreak. A good insecticide is one that effectively reduces the population of pest insects in the target area without simultaneously killing off the other animals that help limit the pest population.

Fighting Nature with Nature

If pests have natural predators, why don't we just use the predators to control the pests? We do. Some candidates for pest control are other animals that have already developed specific relationships with certain insects. This is called living pest control, or biological control. However, living pest control requires using organisms that target the pest in question without collateral damage to the food web—in other words, you want the predator organisms to stick around during periods when the pests are absent but not become pests themselves. It's important to be sure that we don't unleash a new pest in an attempt to control another.

A Delicate Balance

The best animal candidates for biological control include predatory mites (Acari), beetles and wasps, and parasitoid wasps and flies. Predators can be an effective means of control, because most predators consume many prey individuals over a lifetime. Sometimes introducing certain predators, such as ladybugs (Coccinellidae), can temporarily eliminate a population of aphids. With the aphids gone, the ladybugs move on, to seek new prey at

another site, or they die from lack of food. If this occurs, the next season could be just as rife with pests, and the overall effect is negligible. It's important to create a balance between the predators and the pests on which they prey.

Enemies on the Inside

Parasitoids spend their larval development inside or on prey species, consuming and killing them as they grow. Egg parasitoids can be highly effective in dealing with pest species, because they get into the eggs and consume the pests before they even hatch, thereby preventing any damage to host plants. By using natural enemies to control pests, we can avoid using harmful chemical insecticides and introducing new, possibly devastating, species into the environment. A downside is that because the pests and their predators/parasitoids have coexisted for so long, the chances of the pests being completely eliminated are low. Of course, eliminating the pest completely means starving their predators/parasitoids, which then couldn't help out if the pests were ever reintroduced.

Invasion of the Cane Toads!

People have tried for decades to introduce various animals to new environments to control insect pests. There are very few examples of success and plenty of failures. A good example of a failed experiment was the introduction of the Cane toad (Anura: Bufonidae: *Bufo marinus*) in Australia. Cane toads are native to Central and South America but were imported by Australians in the 1930s in an effort to control their native cane beetles (Scarabaeidae: *Dermolepida albohirtum* and *Lepidota frenchi*), which were eating sugar cane crops. The toads would eat the beetles if they encountered them on the ground, but the pest scarabs feed underground as larvae and in the leaves of the sugar cane as adults, which put them out of the toads' reach. In retrospect, the toad was a terrible choice to control the cane beetles, and not enough homework was done before releasing it. Introducing the Cane toad to solve a problem just created a larger problem, as the toads spread across Northeast Australia, disturbing ecosystems by eating and poisoning native species. The cane beetles—the supposed targets—seem to be the only Australian species not affected by the toad's introduction.

Homegrown Heroes

An Australian species of ant known as the Meat ant (*Iridomyrmex reburrus*) is tough, even by Australian standards. As its common name suggests, the Meat ant slaughters other insects and any other small animals that can't get away. Cane toads don't have the escape responses that native frogs do and stand perfectly still, instead of leaping to safety, when the ant butchers arrive. The toads' toxins keep them safe from vertebrate predators but seem to have no effect on marauding ants. The toads are also active during the day and breed in the dry season, when the banks of the ponds are sunbaked mud with little cover. Although adult Cane toads are likely too large to be taken down by the Meat ants, their freshly transformed toadlets make easy pickings along the water's edge. New initiatives are underway to encourage the Meat ants to forage near known Cane-toad breeding areas, in the hope of controlling the invasive species.

Do Your Homework

Most modern examples of animal biological control are better researched than those of the past. Many of the success stories involve an introduced pest being controlled by another introduced species that comes from the same place. By investigating the kinds of insects that feed on the pests back home, we can find a good candidate for biological control. Insects that are picky and eat only one kind of plant or one kind of aphid or only parasitize one kind of caterpillar are the best choices for introduction. Introducing the right species of plant-eating insects could, and has already helped, eliminate many introduced weeds around the world.

Bug Bite

The Spurge hawk moth (Sphingidae: *Hyles euphorbiae*) was introduced from Europe into southern Alberta in the late 1960s, in an attempt to control an invasive weed from Europe and Asia, Leafy spurge (*Euphorbia esula*). Although the caterpillars of this handsome moth eat the weed like it is going out of style, Leafy spurge still persists throughout most of North America. Sometimes more than just one species or method of pest control is needed to be effective.

Encourage Diversity

If a pest causes problems in its own natural habitat, the cause could be that its natural enemies are absent, for some reason. One way to encourage a pest's natural predators is to plant crops near areas that supply predators and parasitoids with habitat and shelter, such as mixed stands of trees, mixed shelterbelts and sections of wild grasses and flowers. Mixing our crops helps reduce potential pest impact and maintains predator harborages. This strategy doesn't guarantee that we'll never need to use chemical pesticides again—but it doesn't hurt to use all of the many natural agents of pest control available to us.

Microbe Allies

Living pest control can also include using microbes, such as bacteria, fungi, viruses and other tiny organisms, such as nematodes. These organisms have longstanding relationships with the pest species and tend to be target specific. Because many of them are already part of the ecosystem, they're not likely to pollute it (as chemical insecticides do); also, the pests are less likely to become resistant to the organisms, largely because the organisms can evolve along with the pests.

Nematodes Versus Insects

Nematodes are a phylum of wormlike animals, some of which are parasites of many different groups of organisms. Those that attack insects are very small and can be reared in large vats and then sprayed like pesticide on crops or pests. They can be ingested by the insect host or burrow in themselves. Because they are possibly the most abundant group of animals on Earth, there is no shortage of them, and there are many potential candidates for insect control.

Glowing Grubs

Heterorhabditidae, a family of nematodes, have symbiotic gut bacteria that actually overcome the host for the nematode. Once inside a host insect larva, the nematodes release the bacteria from their guts; the bacteria go to

People and Pests

work killing the host, digesting the tissues and preventing decomposition. To make an already gruesome situation worse, the bacteria glow! As the bacteria multiply, the insect host takes on eerie, glow-in-the-dark quality. Once the bacteria have done the prep work, the nematode begins to feed—and feed it does. The nematode needs its strength to complete development, which involves becoming a hermaphrodite (male and female at the same time), laying eggs in the insect carcass and retaining some inside its own body.

When they hatch, the young nematodes eat their mother, then mate and lay eggs. Weeks later, the insect body explodes into thousands of nematodes seeking another host. If one grub or caterpillar yields thousands of nematodes, each capable of killing one more insect, using the parasites as pest control can be pretty effective. There are nematodes specific to soil pests and the aquatic larvae of black flies (Diptera: Simuliidae) and mosquitoes, and some even attack the various families of wood-boring beetles.

Deadly Fungus

Fungi are the most common disease organisms affecting insects—though only a few are known to infect species we consider agricultural or medical pests. How do they work? Fungal spores (the fungus equivalent of seeds) float along on the wind and settle on surfaces that insects frequent, where they come in contact with an insect. Once attached to the insect host, the spore germinates and sends out root-like hyphae that push through the exoskeleton and into the host body cavity. The hyphae can release toxins that kill the insect, or they can simply grow to the point where the body is so stuffed with the fungus that it no longer functions. Once dead, the insect is absorbed by the developing fungus, which then goes on to produce more spores to infect the next insect.

Attack of the Zombie Caterpillars

An insect-killing (entomopathic) fungus called *Entomophaga maimaiga*, which means "insect eater," can be sprayed on leaves or soil; when caterpillars and sawflies (Hymenoptera: Symphyta) come in contact with it, they quickly start behaving differently than their uninfected brethren. Most disturbing is that healthy members of the population recognize the infected individuals and run away from them. The infected caterpillars probably don't have the capacity to understand why their relatives are fleeing at the sight of them, but to human observers, the behaviour looks a lot like what you'd see in a zombie movie. Eventually, the infected, fungus-ridden caterpillars climb to the highest point on the tree or branch, well above their brothers and sisters feeding below, and die. The body, which is now packed with fungal spores, starts to leak a thick pink liquid, which drips down onto the leaves and uninfected caterpillars, to start the process all over again.

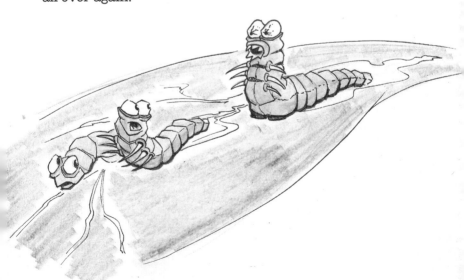

Bacteria Versus Insects

Bacteria can also be used as pest control, though there are fewer bacteria that attack healthy insects than you might expect. Several different species have been used against introduced scarab beetle pests. The most popular by far is *Bacillus thuringiensis* (Bt), originally discovered as the cause of death in Silk-moth caterpillars (Bombycidae: *Bombyx mori*). Bt has many subspecies that are adapted to different conditions and hosts. It can be effective against leaf-feeding caterpillars and mosquito larvae living in water. It works by first being ingested; then its crystal proteins dissolve in the gut, releasing toxins that erode the gut lining, leading to death.

Bt to the Rescue

The Gypsy moth (Lymantriidae: *Lymantria dispar*) was introduced accidentally to North America when a French scientist, Leopold Trouvelot, working in Massachusetts tried to find a disease-resistant source of silk, and some Gypsy moths escaped from his lab. That was in 1868. Within a few years, outbreaks had begun, and the sound of chewing mandibles and falling frass filled the forests of Eastern North America. Millions of acres of trees have been stripped of their leaves in the 140 years since the Gypsy moth was introduced to the New World.

More than 60 different species of predators and parasitoids have been introduced in attempts to stop the moth, which feeds on hundreds of different kinds of plants. Some of the introductions, such as parasitoid Tachinid flies, have turned out to be pests in their own right—and, instead of attacking the Gypsy moths, they have decimated the native giant silk moths (Saturniidae). Bt has proven to be effective against the Gypsy moth and plenty of other forest pests, for that matter. It is found naturally in ecosystems worldwide and is unlikely to become a problem of its own. We just have to apply it in the right places at the right time.

Some groups of insects are also susceptible to other toxins that Bt bears, and a taste is enough to paralyze the insect and stop feeding damage. There are a few drawbacks to using Bt for pest control: the cost of producing large quantities, pests must be feeding at the time to get a dose, it degrades in sunlight and determining the right Bt sub-species to use on the pest in question. Luckily, there are at least 40 different Bt varieties, with different hosts.

The Benefits of Bugs

Bug Food

Although there is probably no group of animals more important to ecosystems on land, most of us don't consider insects to be especially useful. We are so wrong. Insects are beneficial in myriad ways—and one of the most important is the role they play in our food chain. We couldn't eat as well as we do without insects to pollinate our crops, and, whether we eat them intentionally or accidentally, insects are a nutritious and abundant food source. Putting them on the menu for humans or livestock could reduce our ecological footprint and limit the use of chemicals. Ultimately, insects aren't really that different from other arthropods, such as the crab, shrimp and lobster that many of us love to eat. They're just smaller and probably less salty.

Bugs on the Menu

Entomophagy, the practice of eating insects, is actually widespread among humans. It is said that 80 percent of the world's population eats insects on purpose, and the rest of us are just in denial. Why? Because the other 20 percent of us, mostly Europeans and North Americans and anyone considered "westernized," still consume plenty of insects—just not on purpose.

How is that possible, you ask, while contemplating your last meal? Well, because of insects' size and universal presence, any processed foods made from vegetable and other plant sources are bound to contain some proportion of insects. Governments have even established regulations to limit the allowable number of insect fragments per unit weight of food. For example, cheese in Canada is only allowed to contain four insect fragments and 25 dead mites per 225 grams. For the vegetarians out there, tofu can have as many as 65 insect fragments and 15 dead mites per 100 grams. It's okay for ground black pepper to have 200 insect fragments per 50 grams, and 100 grams of mushrooms can include 10 maggots less than 2 millimetres long—no maggots over 2 millimetres are allowed, thankfully. Peanut butter and chocolate place second to black pepper, but I think you get the point. Although you might be disgusted to discover that you've been an insect eater your whole life, now you can appreciate it.

The Benefits of Bugs

Gross But Good for You

Traditional peoples living in South and Central Africa, Asia, Australia and South America commonly consume insects and other terrestrial arthropods. Often cultures that face a seasonal lack of animal protein from other sources supplement their diet with insects. Insects are generally high in protein and energy and are an excellent source of vitamins and minerals, such as calcium, phosphorous, magnesium, iron, zinc, vitamin B, B2 and niacin. Often, the larvae of insects that undergo complete metamorphosis, such as caterpillars and beetle grubs, are full of stored fat, in preparation for pupation.

Fear No Weevil

One of the richest sources of animal fat are the larvae of the Palm weevil (Curculionidae: *Rhynchophorus phoenicis*), which are eaten by people in Africa, Asia and South America. Because Palm weevils are considered pests on coconut and oil palm plantations, perhaps pest control could include serving them to plantation workers for lunch.

Caterpillar Jerky

Caterpillars of the Emperor moth (Saturniidae: *Imbrasia belina*) are eaten in Botswana, Namibia, South Africa and Zimbabwe. The caterpillars are gutted, boiled and dried to make caterpillar jerky that's 50 percent protein and 15 percent fat—almost twice as nutritious as cooked beef! Although caterpillar jerky is not as tasty as barbecued steak, its higher nutritional value is important to people who don't always have much to eat and can't afford to buy meat regularly at the grocery store.

Barbecued Bird Eater

The Piaroa natives in Venezuela capture and roast Goliath bird eaters (Theraphosidae: *Theraphosa blondi*) and other large tarantulas, eating them much the same way other people eat crab and lobster. As do all tarantulas in North and South America, Goliath bird eaters have irritating hairs that they can scratch off their abdomens with a hind leg. These hairs are called urticaria, and their thorny, thistle-like shape helps them dig into the skin and other soft spots of a predator that touches them. Once embedded in the skin, sinuses or eyes, the hairs cause allergic reactions, which get worse with every exposure. The Piaroa have found a way to deal with these urticaria: they're burned off during the barbecue, and the tarantula's fangs are used as toothpicks afterward.

The Benefits of Bugs

Bug Bite

The tarantula's irritating urticaria were the original ingredient in itching powder, a product sold for use as a practical joke. Because the allergic reactions to the tarantula hairs only get worse every time we come in contact with them, the powder was probably a bad idea. Although putting itching powder in someone's socks or underwear might seem like a funny joke, getting urticaria in your eye can actually scar the eyeball if it's not removed immediately.

Bug Burgers, Anyone?

It has been argued that, because insects are "cold-blooded" (their internal body temperature fluctuates with the external temperature), they are more efficient at converting food into body mass. It's true that, compared to mammals such as cows, insects don't waste most of the energy from their diet just maintaining a steady internal temperature. We and our mammal relatives spend almost 90 percent of our energy from food just to keep the furnace warm, at 37°C.

Insects and reptiles allow their body temperature to cool when they're not active, saving energy by lowering the metabolic rate. Because they are far more efficient (as much as 70 percent of their diet becomes tissue) than mammals (cows turn only 3 to 10 percent of their food into tissue), we could raise insect mini-livestock and get more meat per gram of feed than any other domesticated animals. Raising insects also requires less water than raising cattle, even when you compare equal weights of them (3290 litres of water are needed for every 150 grams of beef). The amount of food required to rear one cow can produce 20 times the cow's weight in House crickets (Grillidae: *Acheta domesticus*), in far less time.

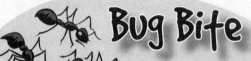

Bug Bite

In some countries, bugs are used to feed animals. Houseflies (*Musca domestica*), Mealworms (*Tenebrio molitor*) and Silkworm (*Bombyx mori*) pupae have been used in China to feed chickens, pigs, fish and mink with great success. Bug feed even costs less than the usual fish-based feeds that are fed to these animals and contribute to overfishing worldwide.

Exoskeleton-eating Enzymes

Chitin, which is a string of sugar molecules (a polysaccharide) containing nitrogen, gives the insect exoskeleton and fungal cell walls strength. Most humans who consume insects as food cannot digest chitin, so it acts like dietary fibre, with all the associated health benefits. Australian Aborigines are the only humans capable of digesting insect exoskeleton, thanks to an enzyme (a molecule that breaks down or builds another) they have, called trehalase. The enzyme helps break down the bonds in the exoskeleton and other parts of the insect body.

Spinning Silk

Silk is a fibre produced for various reasons by many different groups of insects and spiders. It makes a tough waterproof home, is a safe place to transform into an adult and, depending on its shape and stickiness, can be an efficient way to catch dinner.

Waiter, There's a Cocoon in My Tea

The ancient Chinese were the first to turn caterpillar silk into fabrics. Legend has it that Lady Hsi-Ling-Shih, wife of the Yellow Emperor who ruled China in about 3000 BC, was drinking tea one day when a cocoon fell into her cup.

As she removed the cocoon, she noticed that it unravelled easily, and the rest is history. Evidence of even earlier silk production in China exists in the form of spinning tools, silk thread and fabric that might be almost 7000 years old.

Farming Silk

Silk, an organic fibre of incredible strength, is produced commercially by rearing millions of Silk-moth caterpillars, or Silkworms (Bombycidae: *Bombyx mori*). The Silkworms are fed mulberry leaves or commercial Silkworm chow and raised until they build a silk cocoon. Normally, this self-knit sleeping bag would keep the developing Silk moth safe and dry during pupation, until it emerges as an adult. Instead, silk-makers throw the cocoons into boiling water, killing the pupae, and unravel the silk threads. Each cocoon can contain as much as 275 metres of single-stranded silk! These single strands are doubled over on themselves 15 times to make a single woven thread, which is used to weave silk fabrics. Approximately 30,000 Silkworms and a ton of mulberry leaves are needed to produce a little more than 5 kilograms of raw silk.

Bug Bite

A byproduct of the silk farming, or sericulture, industry are the millions of boiled pupae, which are combined with brown sugar and soy sauce and sold in cans. Served with rice and stir-fried vegetables, they are delicious. Not so good cold and raw—trust me, I've tried them.

Spider Silk

Spiders also produce silk, but it's much stronger than Silkworm silk. Spiders have seven different kinds of silk glands, though you will only find three to six glands in any one type of spider. Each of these glands produces a different kind of silk. Possibly the two most common forms of spider silk are the pillow-soft inner layer and the tough, papery outer layer of the spiders' egg cases. Both varieties of egg-case silk come from the same gland—the difference in form is determined by how fast the spider squeezes out the silk and how the spider spins the silk. Some spiders only use their silk to build a special silk package for their eggs. The case cushions the eggs, so they won't crack open, and shelters them from predators and parasitoids so they can't rip through the outer envelope.

Other types of spider silk from different silk glands are the tough rope or sheet-like, prey-binding type; strong and sticky anchoring silk, to keep the web secure; lightweight scaffold silk used temporarily during web construction; super-strong, non-sticky scaffold silk, used to make the web spokes; the sticky liquid droplets; and the sticky web silk that connects the spokes and helps trap prey long enough to be noticed by the spider.

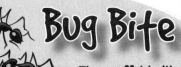

Bug Bite

The scaffold silk produced by large orb-weaver spiders in the family Araneae is five times stronger than steel of the same thickness. If a strand of scaffold silk as thick as a pencil was stretched across the flight path of a Boeing 747 airplane, it could stop the aircraft without breaking! The sticky silk used to connect the spokes of the web and capture prey can stretch two to four times its original length before breaking.

Spider-spun Fish Nets

Traditional hunter-gatherers living in Borneo and Papua-New Guinea have a clever use for orb-weaver spider webs. They find a large orb-weaver (*Nephila maculata*, for example) with a web in need of repair and place a length of reed that has been bent into a vaguely key-shaped loop beside the web. By the next evening, the spider has built a nice new web on the convenient reed frame. The hunters release the spider but keep the loop of reed with the web on it. The silk from the spider is so strong that the webbed loop can be used as a fishing net to pull small- and medium-sized fish from rivers and streams.

Spider Silk Fabric?

Why don't we use spider silk like we do Silk-moth silk? The best reason is the cost of rearing spiders. Silkworms will eat commercial food, which is much easier to provide than live insects, on which the spiders prefer to dine. Housing spiders that can spin webs 2 or 3 metres in diameter can also be a challenge. Lastly, the spiders would need to be wrangled out of their webs and into some contraption that spools silk from them. This has been done, but the silk yield is low compared to that from Silkworms.

Spider-Goats

The genes that spiders carry that allow them to produce silk have been successfully transplanted into goats. The rationale here is that by inducing an easier-to-care-for animal to produce silk of spider quality, we might be able to obtain larger quantities of it. However, the silk-producing glands of the poor mutant goat are different from the those of the spiders', and, apparently, the goat silk comes from the goat's mammary glands. The most obvious drawback here, Frankenstein-ian ethics aside, is that a goat that lactates silk won't be rearing a herd of spider-goats unless they are nursed by normal, milk-producing goats.

Bug Bite

Spider silk is still used today as the crosshairs in the eyepieces of microscopes and the scopes of firearms. If it were ever produced in large enough quantities, spider silk would be more valuable as a component of bulletproof vests than it would as fabric for scarves and handkerchiefs.

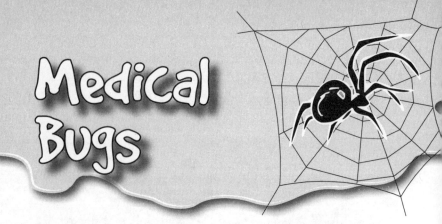

Medical Bugs

Although most of us would prefer not to see bugs in a hospital or anywhere else that medicine is practiced, bugs can be used in surprising ways in the medical field.

The Value of Venom

Many insect and arachnid venoms contain substances that could be medically useful. Using toxins as medicine might seem a little odd, but if the right part of the venom is used in the right place, the effects can be beneficial. Typically, venom is a complex mixture of chemicals and enzymes that have an overall negative effect on the victim. However, some of these substances, when isolated from the other venom components, are helpful in treating certain illnesses and conditions. The venom of the Chilean rose tarantula (*Grammostola spatulata*) has been found to help people suffering from stroke and blood clots by decreasing blood pressure and helping to break down arterial plaque.

Scorpion Yin and Yang

One of the most dangerous scorpions in the world, and certainly the most venomous, is the Israeli deathstalker (Buthidae: *Leiurus quinquestriatus*). A mere 0.16 milligrams of venom per kilogram of mammal is enough to cause death, in most cases, and this species has been known to inject as much as 0.483 milligrams of venom per sting. This means one sting (only two or three drops) can have enough venom to kill 120 mice! The deathstalker's venom isn't all deadly, though. One component of its venom is the chlorotoxin peptide, which has proven highly effective in treating brain tumours. Other substances in the deathstalker's venom might help regulate insulin production for diabetics.

Sting Therapy

Bee and wasp venom can contain biologically active substances, such as adrenaline and histamine. The venom is harmful when taken as a whole, but the individual ingredients can be useful. The most useful application of hymenopteran venom is in immunotherapy, to treat people with severe allergies. It seems crazy, but people who are dangerously allergic to bee and wasp venom appear to be become desensitized to it when they receive small, regular doses of that very venom. The treatment involves injecting small amounts of venom extract daily, then weekly and then monthly for several years. The best news is that the treatment appears to have almost 100 percent success in moderating a formerly life-threatening reaction to a bee sting.

Bug Bite

The dubious award for most deaths caused by being stung, bitten or otherwise filled with venom goes to the Hymenoptera. These deaths are mostly from massive allergic reactions, and two thirds of those human deaths occur within an hour of receiving a single sting. Those of us who are not allergic to bee or wasp stings can still die from them, though: a child receiving more than 50 stings or an adult receiving more than 100 stings all at once is in a life-threatening situation.

The Benefits of Bugs

Bee Bothers

Honeybees (Hymenoptera: Apidae: *Apis mellifera*) are suffering from a number of insults these days. In North America, beekeepers (apiarists) can make more money renting their pollinating bees to orchardists than they can by selling honey. The lack of interest in honey means there's less incentive to keep bees that produce large amounts of honey, which is a sign of a healthy, widely foraging colony. Perhaps we've forgotten just how useful honey really is. Although honey is the best-known bee product, beeswax is also useful, as an ingredient in lipstick, ointment, crayons, candy and baking and for waterproofing, candle making, bronze preservation, polish for ironwork, lubricants for metalworking drills and saws, and even jewellery.

A World of Uses

Honey is possibly the most useful substance that bees have provided us with. Honey has been used as medicine for thousands of years by human societies around the world.

- Egyptians—The Smith Papyrus, a copy of an Egyptian medical text dating to 1700 BC, describes the treatment of wounds and infections related to battle, in particular a treatment using a coagulated milk-and-honey mixture, which was packed into and around a wound. The milk-and-honey treatment was not exclusive to the ancient Egyptians; it was also used in some form by East African tribes, the Romans, American Indigenous people and even rural communities in the American South.

- Muslims—In Islam, bees are seen as gifts from Allah, not only for their role in pollinating the plants on which our livestock feed but also for the healing honey that they produce.

- Chinese—Traditional Chinese medicine draws heavily on honey, whether taken internally or as a topical wound and burn treatment.

- Aztecs—The ancient Aztecs used salted honey and the sugary sap of a species of agave (Agavaceae: *Agave americana*), which has been shown in modern times to have antibiotic properties.

- Mexicans—In Mexican folk medicine, a mix of sugar and honey, with its ridiculously high concentration of sugars, is used as an antibiotic ointment for open infections.

Healing with Honey

Even as recently as the 1970s, doctors from the Ukraine, Russia, Germany and Saudi Arabia have found medical uses for honey, including treating ailments of the ear, nose, throat, eye, skin and urethra and even for shingles infections. In India, it was used to treat leprosy; in New Zealand and Australia, honey was used for abdominal infections and ulcers. Surgeons have found that honey solutions can preserve blood vessels, corneas and bones long enough for transplants to be performed. The process of storing live tissues in honey is called mellitization. Honey and sugar solutions seem to preserve and protect tissues from infection in the same way that sugary fruit combinations, such as jam, jellies and other preserves, resist bacteria and fungi.

Sweet Treatment

Because honey is essentially nectar that has been processed by bees to remove most of the water content, it has a tendency to draw water to it. This is also true of dry crystalline sugar. A paste of combined sugar and honey applied to open wounds draws liquids from infected tissues. Drying the muscles can help the healing process (the same reason you want clean, dry bandages), and the sugar-honey concoction can actually aid in muscle repair.

French physicians Jean Louis Trouillet and Jean Chastre found that sugar pastes are effective healing promoters within the body, as well. Chest cavities packed with this paste drastically reduced healing times in patients recovering from heart surgery from 85 days to about 50. In India, caesarean-section incisions that were coated with honey and then taped were less painful and healed quicker than wounds treated with the usual dressings and stitches.

Sweet Success

Dr. Leon Herszage, an Argentine surgeon, published results of a 1980 study gauging the effectiveness of using sterilized sugar pastes to treat surgical wounds. The recovery rate was greater than 99 percent. In Mississippi, Dr. Richard Knutson treated burns, gunshot wounds, ulcers and amputations with a sugar and iodine paste; he published a five-year study of hundreds of patients; 98 percent of them experienced complete healing. Not only did patients treated with sugar and honey heal more completely with less scarring, they also did so very quickly. In comparison, standard medical treatments demonstrate a 94-percent success rate.

Undoing Ulcers

Stomach ulcers are the painful erosion of the stomach's mucus lining by the actions of *Helicobacter pylori*, a bacteria found in the stomach. Honey, when concentrated and taken in large enough doses, can kill the ulcer-causing bacteria and is far more effective than antacids and other modern treatments.

Killer Honey

Through research, scientists have found that honey can kill bacteria such as pneumococci, streptococci, staphylococci and *Escherichia coli* and those causing typhoid, dysentery, tuberculosis and leprosy—all of which are dangerous and extremely common around the world. Both honey and sugar appear to boost immune response by white blood cells (leukocytes), which absorb and kill germs in the body. The sugar and honey preparations also absorb the water from the invading organisms and damaged cells, which shrivels them up. Healthy cells can compensate by absorbing more water from the blood or lymphatic systems and actually feed on the sugar, potentially explaining the quick healing times.

Honey: It's a Good Thing

Sugar isn't the only ingredient in honey. Honey also contains hydrogen peroxide, the same stuff that drugstores sell as an antiseptic and that your white blood cells use to kill germs and other intruders. Another antibiotic substance in honey is formic acid, which is used by wood ants (Hymenoptera: Formicidae: *Formica* spp.) to rub into the bites they inflict with their jaws. Formic acid is used to flavour many sour candies. Honey has vitamin C (ascorbic acid) and small amounts of iron, magnesium, copper, phosphorus, sodium, potassium, manganese and calcium, which are vital substances that help repair damaged cells and tissues in the body. It's possible that honey contains growth factors, which explains the rapid healing of scars and infections. However, because sterile sugar pastes have been used with similar success, it could be that honey is simply a cheap, self-preserving and relatively sterile source of sugar for traditional people the world over.

Before you rush off to slather your scrapes in honey, however, consider that honey processing and packaging can introduce certain harmful bacteria (*Clostridium botulinum*, for instance, the agent of botulism). As yet, there are no sterile, medical-grade honeys on the market, possibly because of the lack of published scientific evaluation of traditional medicines. This is changing slowly, however.

Other Bug Benefits

Traditional peoples around the world have used insects and spiders in practices that are thousands of years old, representing ancient techniques that have almost disappeared. However, some insect substances, such as chitin, are still useful today. Although the traditional survival methods used by such groups are diminishing, we can only hope that this ancient way of life might carry on somewhere.

Bugs to Dye For

Cochineal insects (Hemiptera: Coccoidea: *Dactylopius coccus*), which feed on prickly pear cacti, are a natural source of red dye. South Americans have used Cochineal insects as dye since well before European contact. Another scale insect (*Kerria lacca*) is processed into a commercial varnish called shellac. Considering the number of potentially useful species of insects, there are very few domesticated ones.

Poison Bugs, Frogs and Darts

Poison dart frog toxin, called batrachotoxin, is the most potent natural toxin ever discovered. One tiny Golden dart frog (Dendrobatidae: *Dendrobates terribilis*) has enough toxins to kill 50 people or tip 50 poison darts. What's exceptional about the toxin is that the frogs obtain it from their diet of poisonous Melyrid beetles and Oribatid mites, so the most poisonous animal in the world owes it all to the bugs it eats. Dart frogs raised in captivity don't seem to be able to produce these toxins, or, if they do, not in such quantities.

Bug Bite

A common misconception is that Central Americans use poison dart frog toxin as an ingredient in recipes that induce a dreamlike state for spiritual journeys, but this is not true. These substances are actually obtained from certain toads (Bufonidae) and some species of tree frogs (Hylidae), not dart frogs.

Useful Chitin

The tough polysaccharide in insect exoskeleton, called chitin, resists many kinds of chemicals. In addition to being a food source for traditional Australian Aborigines, chitin has been used as a clotting agent to help heal wounds, as a means of lowering cholesterol in the blood and as a non-allergenic drug carrier. It can also be used to filter pollution from water bodies and can even be made into a biodegradable plastic.

Bug Bite

Male Giant spiny stick insects (*Eurycantha horrida*) have 2-centimetre-long spurs on the underside of their rear femora (singular: femur, the upper part of the leg), which they use to stab would-be predators. Indigenous New Guineans use the spurs as fishing hooks for their fishing lines.

Mythology: Ancient and Modern

Ancient Myths

We haven't always despised insects—many ancient cultures even revered them. Some earned our respect and appreciation through the roles they performed, such as providing honey. Others were revered because we gave them attributes that they did not actually have, such as good luck or protection from evil spirits. Because so much archaeology and research has been done in Egypt, the ancient Egyptian's veneration of cats and other animals, such as insects, is well understood.

Sacred Scarabs

The honoured Egyptian insect that's probably the most well known is the scarab beetle, which was personified by the sun god Khepri, who was associated with resurrection and new life. Much of this reverence for the scarab beetle is based in the similarity between Egyptian beliefs and the scarabs beetles' habits. Egyptians believed the sun was rolled across the sky, for example, in much the same way as a scarab beetle rolls a ball of dung across the ground.

They also saw similarities in the dung beetles' lifecycle and believed that the beetles created themselves from balls of dung. Of course the beetles don't create themselves from dung, it only appears that way. A dung beetle's lifecycle starts with one or both parents burying the collected dung balls and laying an egg in each of them. As the dung decomposes, it grows fungus, which feeds the developing larvae. Underground, the young beetles pupate and emerge as winged adults, ready to fly off into the world.

This lifecycle has many similarities to the Egyptian ideas of burial and rebirth in the afterlife; their tombs are similar to the underground brood chambers from which the beetles fly. Emerging from underground, the adult scarab seem to be springing from nothingness or are even being reborn, much as the Egyptians believed they would be after death.

Bug Bite

Between 2345 and 30 BC, amulets carved to resemble scarabs were used as royal seals.

Trapped in Trees

Wood-boring beetles in the family Buprestidae were also depicted in tombs and on jewellery. Their larvae feed on the wood and softer tissues of trees, a lifestyle that also parallels Egyptian mythology. Osiris, lord of the afterlife and underworld, was tricked by his brother, Seth, and trapped inside a tree. When Isis, the goddess of mother-hood and fertility, split the tree open, Osiris was reborn, much as the beetle grubs are exposed when trees are split into timber.

Bees and Beetles

Click beetles (Elateridae) have been carved as symbols of the goddess Neith and depicted holding the sacred *waas* sceptre of the gods. Neith was also associated with honeybees, which, according to some Egyptian myths, were the tears of Ra, the sun god. Depictions of beekeeping were seen on temple walls as early as 2445 BC, and pots with inscriptions indicating that they contained honey were found in Tutankh-amen's tomb. Egyptians used honey as a base for medicinal ointments and as food. Beeswax was used as a form for metal casting and as a varnish or paint.

Flies and Locusts

Flies were thought to provide protection against misfortune and disease and were also used as symbols on amulets that were awarded, like medals, to brave soldiers. The fly characteristics revered by the Egyptians must have been their stubborn persistence and refusal to retreat—not behaviours that endeared them to many others.

Locusts, despite being the eighth plague unleashed by God to convince the Pharaoh to release the enslaved Israelites in Exodus, were not a major symbol in Egyptian mythology, except as an indication of large numbers of things. They are found carved into wedding gifts, sarcophagi and temple walls, possibly just as an adjective to describe plenty. Often, the enemy soldiers encountered in battle are indicated by the locust symbol, meaning that there were many of them.

Scorpion Protectors

Scorpions were also commonly depicted in Egypt. Seven scorpions protected Isis, and amulets bearing scorpions and centipedes (for the god Sepa) were intended to ward off venomous animals and enemies of the gods. The goddess Serket, protector of tombs and coffins, had a scorpion on her head. Her name apparently refers to the breath of life and also to whispers on the wind, to which scorpions seem to respond. Scorpions don't see very well, but they are extremely sensitive to vibration and air movement, thanks to whisker-like hairs called trichobothria that cover their pincers (chelae), legs and tail (metasoma). Because of this sensitivity, a scorpion reacting to a breeze or a breath can appear to be aware of something we are not.

Singing Spies

Most singing insects have, by virtue of their songs, made their way into human myths. The Greeks believed that the buzzing cicadas (Hemiptera: Cicadidae) were reborn human revellers, transformed by the muses to sing their whole lives without the need for food. The cicadas listened to people's conversations and, when they died, reported back to the muses on the habits and fidelity of those they had overheard. Cicadas' activities after death are as unknown as any other organism's, but they most certainly do need food to survive. The Chinese in the Chou and Haan dynasties also believed that cicadas never ate and only drank dew. They buried their dead with jade cicadas in their mouths to ensure everlasting life. Singing insects were often compared to chanting Buddhist monks and priests.

Bug Bite

Predatory katydids (Orthoptera: Tettigoniidae) were kept as game animals in China and other parts of Asia to fight one another in contests. The katydid was considered a symbol of strength and ferocity.

Mantid Mystics

Mantids were associated with courage and fearlessness. The Khoisan people, indigenous to southern Africa, tell stories of mantids taking on the role of trickster, a character commonly attributed to the fox or raven in European and North American folklore. The Xam Bushmen (one of many Khoisan groups) call this mantid Kaggen and consider him responsible for the creation of the moon, the animals and the behaviour of humans. Also capable of reviving the dead and transforming into other animals, Kaggen rescued porcupine from her murderous father, Khwai-hem, the All-Devourer, and she bore a son, the *Ichneumon* wasp, who aided and advised his friend, the mantid.

Some ethnologists doubt that the name Kaggen refers to God and also to the mantids, believing that Europeans mistranslated the Xam stories. It's likely that the term refers to both, because mantids were seen as oracles, one and the same with the Gods they channel. Usually there is little distinction between a divine being and the animals associated with them, the latter being seen as manifestations of the former on Earth. In Greek, the word "mantis" means prophet or seer, the mantid's huge compound eyes staring presumably into the future. Even the common name we're most familiar with, the Praying mantis, is a Christian term that refers to the mantid's raptorial forelimbs clasped in a prayer-like manner.

Inspiring Spider

In Scottish folklore, Robert the Bruce, King of Scots from 1306 to 1329, was apparently inspired by the efforts of a spider he observed while hiding from the English after an unsuccessful battle. Each time the spider tried to string a web between two points on the ceiling of the barn (or house, depending on who's telling the story), it failed. As the story goes, the spider never gave up and managed to bridge the gap with silk on its eighth attempt. Robert the Bruce took this to heart and defeated England to free Scotland on his own eighth time around, at the battle of Bannockburn in 1314.

Minute Motivator

Tamerlane (also known as Timur), the famous Mongol-Turkic ruler in Persia between 1370 and 1405, was apparently motivated by the actions of a tiny ant. After his mighty army was defeated, he fled into the wilderness, where he observed an ant trying to carry a grain of wheat larger than itself up a tree and into a hole. The ant slipped and fell 20 times before succeeding, giving Tamerlane the hope that he too might succeed in his impossible task of creating a central Asian empire on par with that of his Mongol ancestors. This, like the story of Robert the

Bruce and the spider, are older versions of the phrase "if at first you don't succeed, try and try again," a story that has been played out since the dawn of life. Selection favours resilience.

Saved by a Spider, Helped by a Hornet

In Jewish folk stories, young David encountered predatory hornets and spiders building webs and saw no use for them. He asked Yahweh (God): "Why did you make the destructive hornets and spiders that weave silk we cannot wear?" To which Yahweh replied: "Do you mock the things I have created? A day will come when you will need them, and then you will know why they were created." Years later, after defeating Goliath and countless armies, David was pursued by King Saul's soldiers for having married the king's daughter, making him a threat to the throne. He ducked into a cave, frightened for his life. There, he watched as a large spider quickly spun a web across the cave entrance. When the soldiers arrived, they took the untouched web as a sign of the cave's emptiness and carried on. David, who, at this point, saw the importance of all creatures, kissed the spider and thanked God accordingly.

Some time later, David was lurking near Saul's tent and was momentarily trapped by sleeping Abner's bent legs. David, frightened that Saul would finally capture him, asked why God had forsaken him. At that moment, a hornet came and stung Abner, causing his legs to straighten, releasing David. So, another apparently useless creature saved David, teaching us that no organism is expendable or worthy of contempt.

Modern Misconceptions

There's no shortage of ancient myths and stories involving insects and spiders, but what about modern myths? Most of the modern misconceptions regarding insects and spiders stem from the media, but they can also be spread by word of mouth, as "old wives' tales" and urban myths.

Earwigs in Your Ear

Earwigs (Dermaptera) were given their English name, either because of the ear-like shape of the hind wings or because of an old wives' tale about them crawling into people's ears. The Latin or scientific name for the order means "skin-wings," which refers to their leathery forewings; the English name is thought to derive from "ear-insect" or "ear-wiggler" in Old English. Although some earwig species in Africa inhabit the fur of bats and rodents, they're likely feeding on sloughed skin and secretions or even eating ectoparasites. You're not likely to find an earwig in your ear, or any animal's, for that matter, any more often than any other insect.

Hoaxes about earwigs have circulated on the Internet; these look like a public service announcement from the Texas Department of Agriculture, warning people that, once an earwig gets into your ear, you have two weeks before they pierce your eardrum, lay eggs and devour your brain. The announcement describes how they feed and pupate in the brain before emerging through the nose of the dead host. Before you go running for the earplugs, rest easy; you have nothing to worry about. For one thing, earwigs do not undergo complete metamorphosis, so no pupation ever takes place. Second, and most importantly, even if an earwig accidentally entered your ear, it would certainly never bore into the brain. I think someone watched *Star Trek: The Wrath of Khan*—in which an earwig-like alien is allowed to crawl into someone's brain via the ear—one too many times. If you ever wake up with an earwig wriggling in your ear, remember that it's lost, not trying to bore into your brain, and consider cleaning your ears more thoroughly. If your ears bear any resemblance to normal earwig burrows in the dirt, it might be time to invest in some cotton swabs.

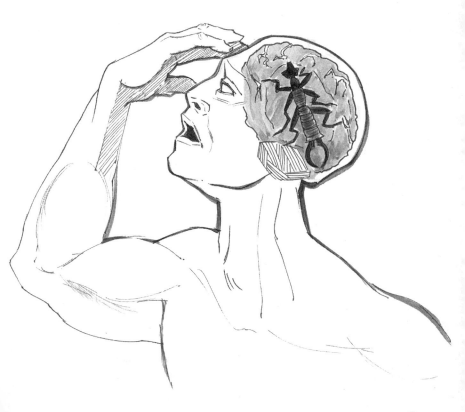

Another common misconception is that "daddy longlegs" are highly venomous but lack fangs long enough to pierce human skin. First of all, let's determine what animal is being referred to as "daddy longlegs." In some parts of the world, the term is used for long-legged crane flies, members of the family Tipulidae. If you've seen what look like mosquitoes on steroids hanging around in shady, damp areas, these are crane flies. They do not drink blood, thankfully, and some adults have not even developed working mouthparts because they stored enough energy from the food they ate as larvae.

Daddy Longlegs #2

Another "daddy longlegs" is the Cellar spider, a member of the Pholcid family (*Pholcus phalagioides*), which, like most spiders, produces venom. Although their chelicerae (fangs) are long enough to break the skin, the venom is not harmful to humans. The female will shake her web violently if disturbed, which is rather unsettling to watch, like a kid throwing a temper tantrum. The Cellar spider is very common in basements and crawlspaces in Eastern North America, South America, Europe, North and South Africa, Southeast Asia and Eastern Australia. The female's body is usually less than 2 centimetres long, and its leg span might reach 7 centimetres. They do well in human homes because they catch and eat insects and other spiders, a service they provide in exchange for shelter. This is true of all spiders that venture indoors; they pay rent by eating other invertebrates that would be more harmful to your home than they are. Remember that spiders do not eat peanut butter sandwiches; they only go for living prey, so they wouldn't live long in your house if there weren't insects to devour.

Mythology: Ancient and Modern

Daddy Longlegs #3

Finally, we have the "daddy longlegs" that belongs to an arachnid group known as harvestmen. These spider relatives are not spiders at all but their own unique order of arachnids called Opiliones. Like spiders, they have eight legs, but their abdomen (opisthosoma) and cephalothorax (prosoma) are fused into one major body segment, and they have no silk glands, nor do they produce venom. Harvestmen are predators that feed on very small insects and other invertebrates. Some are certainly capable of biting humans, but, without venom, they aren't especially dangerous. Their mouthparts differ from those of spiders, and they actually tear their food into small pieces, like scorpions, instead of feeding by piercing and sucking, like spiders. If you look carefully at the next harvestman you see, you'll find that it has only two simple eyes, not the six or eight normally found in spiders.

Ladybug Pee

Ladybugs, or ladybird beetles, as they are called, belong to the Coccinellidae family. They feed mostly on soft-bodied aphids and mites that attack plants. Ants protect the aphids to feed on the honeydew the herbivores produce. Because the ladybugs eat aphids, they are not welcomed by the ants, which do their best to remove the beetle cattle-rustlers. The beetles have a trick up their sleeve, however—when the ants attack, ladybugs tuck their legs underneath the body, so only the knees are exposed. From their knees, they squeeze a nasty-tasting yellow liquid that people often mistake for ladybug pee. The liquid isn't pee but hemolymph, which contains harmful alkaloid chemicals that burn the ant's eyes and mouthparts. Ants that get a dose of the stuff immediately stop what they are doing and try to clean it off before any serious damage is done.

This reflex bleeding also deters birds and other predators, which learn to avoid the bright reds, oranges and yellows with dark spots and stripes that the beetles wear, just as they avoid the Monarch and Viceroy butterflies. In various European cultures, an encounter with a Coccinellid is considered good luck or a chance to make a wish.

Ladybug Age Spots

Another misconception about ladybugs is that the number of spots they have indicates age. This is not true. Beetles undergo complete metamorphosis from larva to adult and stop moulting when they reach adulthood. To add spots as they age, they would need to moult. So, what do the number of spots tell us? They're an indication of the species of ladybug. Adult Two-spotted ladybugs (*Adalia bipunctata*) have two spots on their elytra, regardless of age, just as adult Seven-spotted ladybugs (*Coccinella septempunctata*) have seven and adult Thirteen-spotted ladybugs (*Hippodamia tridecimpunctata*) have 13. In fact, most ladybugs only live about a year or two.

Forest Beetles in Oil Country

One of my favourite modern misconceptions involves the White-spotted sawyer, or Spruce sawyer beetle, *Monochamus scutellatus* (Cerambycidae), also known in Alberta as the "Tar sands beetle." These beetles bore into dead spruce trees to lay eggs that hatch into wood-eating larvae. After pupating under the bark of the dead spruce, the adults emerge and fly off to find a mate and another tree. They are attracted to the scent of dead trees and the terpenoid chemicals they exude. Another source of terpenoids is crude oil, which, you could say, is really just very old dead-tree juice. The beetles are attracted to this scent and flock to oil derricks and oil sands operations such as those found in Fort McMurray, Alberta.

If the only upright, tree-like objects in the vicinity of the delicious-smelling terpenoids are people, the beetles will land and try to bore into you. This has led to quite a number of stories about where the beetles came from and why they attack rig workers. My favourite, by far, is that the beetles have been under the earth with the crude oil for the last few hundred million years and only emerge when we drill and bring the oil to the surface. That would make quite a horror-movie plot, but it's simply not true. More likely, these longhorn beetles head for large oil drilling and tar sands sites because the crude oil smells stronger than the dead spruce trees. Unfortunately, they won't find the suitable habitat they're looking for and will either die or eventually head elsewhere. The good news is that the beetles can't develop inside humans, despite what some oil patch workers might tell you.

Wash Your Face, or the Roaches Will

Cockroaches are possibly the most famous scavengers of the insect world, preferring dead anything to meals that must be captured and subdued. They will eat one another if they find a freshly moulted colleague and are hungry for protein, but they can only do this when the exoskeleton of the unfortunate roach victim is still soft. Their mouthparts are designed to bite and chew soft plants, fungi and other compost, not for tearing through your skin. A cockroach in your home will happily eat the crumbs off your face as you sleep, but it won't bite you. All the more reason to wash your face before bed.

Not-So-Killer Bees

Killer bees are a favourite for the fear-monger, low-budget-horror-movie makers, but most people don't know that much about them. Killer bees are just a subspecies of the European honeybee (*Apis mellifera scutellata*) and were created by breeding the African honeybee (*Apis mellifera adansonii*) with the Common honeybee (*Apis mellifera mellifera*). They were introduced in Brazil in 1956 in an attempt to make tougher honeybees for beekeepers in South America. They are also referred to as Africanized or Brazilian honeybees. One day, in 1957, someone went around to all the experimental hives and removed the special grate-like queen excluders. With nothing to hold the hybrid honeybee queens back, they flew off with their entire colonies in a process called absconding. From Brazil, they have spread across the continent and north-ward through Central America and southern parts of North America, including Mexico, New Mexico, Arizona, California and south Texas.

Killer bees are no more venomous than your average honeybee; a hundred stings are still required to threaten your life. What makes them more dangerous than regular bees is their aggression level. Africanized bees are more sensitive to movement and activity near the hive and will respond in larger numbers to smaller amounts of their own attack pheromones. In other words, they have a shorter temper and will bring a larger posse of sisters to a fight.

This aggression has served the African honeybee well in their home environment, where raiding Honey badgers (Mustelidae: *Mellivora capensis*) can consume a colony's entire store of honey and the larvae inside the honeycombs if the bees don't defend them effectively.

Movie Mistakes

Unfortunately, the majority of what people learn about insects and other arthropods is through the media. Television and movies have done far more damage than good when it comes to the average person's attitudes toward insects and spiders. Ironically, the exotic insects, scorpions and spiders most often used in television and film are quite docile, which makes them great candidates for working with actors.

Killer Cockroaches and Skeletonizing Scarabs

Insects that will eat you either from the outside in or the inside out are a staple of horror movies and made-for-television schlock. There are insects that will enter living tissue and feed upon you and other animals but never more than a few at a time—certainly not enough to devour you completely. Thanks to an episode of the television series *X-Files* and movies such as *The Mummy* (1999), many people of all ages seem to think that cockroaches and scarab beetles will burrow into your flesh or skeletonize fleeing victims in a full sprint. This has made for some entertaining scenarios, but it's not based in fact. Scarab beetles eat dung, fungus, nectar, sap and vegetable matter—not humans.

Deadly Bees

Despite what films such as *The Deadly Bees* (1967), *The Swarm* (1978) and *Killer Bees!* (1974 and 2002) would have you believe, there have been relatively few bee-related deaths since the arrival of the Africanized bees. In Texas, for example, the number of people who die every year from bee stings has not increased since the killer bees showed up in 1990, and, in Mexico, several dozen people have died from killer bee attacks since 1986. In the United States, an average of 40 to 50 reported deaths are caused by hymenopterans every year, though the number might be closer to 200. Although this sounds like a lot of deaths, you're more likely to die from an allergic reaction to penicillin or be struck by lightning than you are to be killed by bees.

What *is* scary about killer bees is that they could be a less human-friendly competitor for the already dwindling Common honeybee. Killer bees produce less honey and are more difficult to manage than their docile domesticated counterparts, so they won't be saving the apiculture industry or providing medicinal honey to those they have stung.

Tarantula Truth

Among my favourite series of movies are the *Indiana Jones* films directed by Steven Spielberg. In the opening scenes of *Raiders of the Lost Ark* (1981), actor Harrison Ford walks into a cave through massive spider webs to emerge with a number of Mexican red-kneed tarantulas (*Brachypelma smithi*) on his back. Of course, this tarantula species is found in the desert, not in the tropical jungle setting in which they're portrayed. Tarantulas don't spin catching webs, like the ones Indiana Jones walked through, either.

Timid Terrors

Why does the Mexican red-knee seem to be the go-to tarantula for so many films? For one thing, they were the first tarantulas to become popular as pets, which led to their eventual status as endangered species, thanks to over-harvesting by unscrupulous collectors. They are also very docile and will not bite unless provoked, such as if you attempted to crush one. The very reason Mexican red-kneed and other tarantulas are used in films is that they do not bite the actors. But they're portrayed as deadly, so people fear them. They are large and hairy, a quality that does not endear them to arachnophobic people, but some of the nicest spiders I have ever met were tarantulas.

Bug Bite

In the 1977 film *Kingdom of the Spiders*, actor William Shatner was up against 5000 (wild-caught) tarantulas that had run out of food, thanks to our overuse of insecticides, and turned to eating livestock and people instead.

Hairdryers: a Goliath Bird Eater's Nightmare

In Amblin Entertainment's 1990 film, *Arachnophobia*, a small American town is terrified by more than 300 *Delena cancerides*, the Flat huntsman spider and at least one Goliath bird eater (*Theraphosa blondi*). The spider cast members are not the sort that many would care to encounter, though all are unlikely to strike unless provoked. The Goliath bird eater is an ornery species that can be tamed with regular handling, provided you start when the spider is young. The one in the film that ran up actor Jeff Daniels' leg only did so because it was being chased with a hairdryer. That's right, the largest spider in the world can be fended off with hot air and will only attack you if it is cornered or you stick your arm down its burrow. Unlike earlier films, the spiders were not actually squashed underfoot—little mustard packages, like the ones you get at fast food restaurants, were used to simulate the gut splatter.

Eight-Legged Fakes

Another movie that portrays spiders is *Eight-Legged Freaks* (2002). In it, spiders fed contaminated insects from a local swamp become enormous and attack the town. About the only piece of factual information about spiders this film has to offer, other than the number of legs, is that spiders are arachnids. In yet another movie that does more to ruin human-arthropod relations, we see very few real spiders compared to computer-generated fiends that fill the bulk of the plot.

Eight-Legged Facts

Notice that no real spiders attack anyone in any of these spider horror movies. If a tarantula does appear on screen biting a person, it is either a hilarious fake or a digital effect. No tarantula is capable of killing a person; tarantula venom is used to digest the internal tissues of prey that must be approximately the same size or smaller than the spider. Even the Goliath bird eater, with the largest venom glands of any spider, does not carry enough venom to digest even a small child. Tarantulas are also so sensitive to vibration that they can easily tell, when you approach, that you're much larger than anything they would normally eat for dinner. If you ever spot a tarantula in the wild, it is usually because the spider hoped you would pass by without noticing or because you approached on tiptoe. It will retreat into its burrow or silken hide at the slightest sign of danger.

Leaping... Tarantulas?

In movies, tarantulas are often shown leaping into the air toward people. This is yet another myth; tarantulas can lunge forward, and arboreal (tree-dwelling) species will leap downward onto prey or parachute to safety with legs outstretched, but none can actually spring directly upward. When you see a tarantula flying across the room to bite someone's jugular, it is almost certainly a fake that has been hurled into frame by someone off-camera. The next time you see a tarantula in a movie, note whether the real spider is ever shown attacking someone. You'll find that the spider, almost always a Mexican red-kneed tarantula, just walks slowly across something, with suspenseful music to add effect.

Which Bug Does Not Belong?

The 1984 film *Indiana Jones and the Temple of Doom* used a number of insects and centipedes in the cave deathtrap scene. As actress Kate Capshaw reaches into a crevice to throw a switch and save her costars, we see all manner of invertebrates just hanging around in the muck. These include House crickets (*Acheta domestica*), likely native to Asia; Madagascar hissing cockroaches (*Gromphadorhina portentosa*); a beautiful Harlequin longhorn beetle (*Acrocinus longimanus*) from Central America; Macleay's specter stick insects (*Extatosoma tiaratum*), from Australia and New Guinea; and a giant centipede (*Scolopendra* sp.), which might be the only creature in the whole scene actually from India, the setting of the scene. Of those, the only remotely dangerous invertebrate is the centipede, which is only seen crawling under the hair of a mannequin, not Kate Capshaw's tresses. The centipede is also the only potential cave dweller among the international arthropod cast—so don't take movies as a source of information about animals.

Grain of Truth

The most recent instalment in the *Indiana Jones* series, *Kingdom of the Crystal Skull* (2008), is not without invertebrates. In one scene, Harrison Ford remarks that small scorpions are more dangerous than large ones, which is a reasonable rule of thumb, considering that most stings occur because the victim didn't notice the scorpion until it was too late. It isn't always true, though the largest and longest scorpions, the Emperor (*Pandinus imperator*) and Flat rock (*Hadogenes troglodytes*) scorpions are no more venomous or dangerous to people than bees. The Israeli Deathstalker (*Leiurus quinquestriatus*) is actually a good-sized scorpion and is extremely dangerous, and the Northern Scorpion (*Paruroctonus boreus*) is tiny and stings no worse than a hornet.

When real animals are involved in a movie, they are usually less dangerous than the plot suggests. Remember that these insects are actors. Stunt doubles aren't usually called in for bug or tarantula scenes because these insects are almost always chosen for their fearsome looks and mild manners.

More Places to Learn About Bugs

Books

Barnard, A. *Hunters and Herders of Southern Africa A Comparative Ethnography of the Khoisan Peoples*. New York: Cambridge University Press, 1992.

Berdichevsky, M. Bin Gorion, M. Bin Gorion, E. Ben-Amos, D., and Lask, I. Mimekor Yisrael. *Selected Classical Jewish Folktales*. Bloomington, IN: Indiana University Press, 1991.

Brunet, B. *Australian Insects: A Natural History*. Sydney, Australia: Reed New Holland, 2000.

Brunet, B. *The Silken Web: A Natural History of Australian Spiders*. Sydney, Australia: Reed New Holland, 1994.

Campbell, N. *Biology*, 4th ed. Menlo Park: The Benjamin/Cummings Publishing Company, 1996.

Carroll, R. *Vertebrate Paleontology and Evolution*. New York: W.H. Freeman and Company, 1988.

Carwardine, M. *Extreme Nature*. London: Harper Collins Publishers, 2005.

Gill, F. *Ornithology*, 2nd ed. New York: W.H. Freeman and Company, 1995.

Grimaldi, D. and Engel, M. *Evolution of the Insects.* New York: Cambridge University Press, 2005.

Gullan, P. and Cranston, P. *The Insects: An Outline of Entomology,* 2nd ed. Oxford: Blackwell Science, 2000.

Krohne, D. *General Ecology,* 2nd ed. Pacific Grove, CA: Brooks/Cole, 2001.

McGavin, G. *Insects, Spiders, and Other Terrestrial Arthropods.* New York: Dorling Kindersley Inc. 2002.

Meier, J. and White, J. (eds.) *Clinical Toxicology of Animal Venoms and Poisons.* New York: CRC Press, 1995.

Mullen, G. and Durden, L. (eds.) *Medical and Veterinary Entomology.* New York: Academic Press, 2002.

Nowak, R. (ed.) *Walker's Mammals of the World,* Vol. I, 6th ed. Baltimore: The Johns Hopkins University Press, 1999.

Pechenik, J. *Biology of the Invertebrates,* 4th ed. New York: McGraw-Hill Higher Education, 2000.

Preston-Mafham, R. and Preston-Mafham, K. *The Encyclopedia of Land Invertebrate Behaviour.* Cambridge, MA: The MIT Press, 1993.

Randall, D. Burggren, W. and French, K. Eckert. *Animal Physiology: Mechanisms and Adaptations,* 5th ed. New York: W.H. Freeman and Company, 2002.

Root-Bernstein, R. and Root-Bernstein, M. *Honey, Mud, Maggots and Other Medical Marvels.* London: Macmillan Publishers, 1999.

Shaw, I. and Nicholson, P. *British Museum Dictionary of Ancient Egypt.* London: British Museum Press, 1995.

Tait, N. (ed.) *Bugs.* San Francisco: Fog City Press, 2005.

Thain, M. and Hickman, M. *The Penguin Dictionary of Biology,* 10th ed. Toronto: Penguin Books Canada, 2001.

Wilson, D. and Reeder, D. (eds.) *Mammal Species of the World,* 3rd ed. Baltimore: Johns Hopkins University Press, 2005.

Websites

Bug Guide for North American insects and spiders, www.bugguide.net

Government of Canada, Health Protection Guidelines for the General Cleanliness of Food: An Overview. 1999. www.hc-sc.gc.ca

Insect Identification Organization, www.insectidentification.org

Integrated Taxonomic Information System, www.itis.gov/

Monarch Watch, The Kansas Biological Survey, University of Kansas, www.monarchwatch.org

What's That Bug website, www.whatsthatbug.com.

University of Florida Book of Insect Records, www.ufbir.ifas.ufl.edu/

About the Author

Peter Heule

Peter Heule's lifelong fascinations with all animals has led to years of experience in the captive husbandry of mammals, reptiles, amphibians, fish and invertebrates. Peter began working at the Royal Alberta Museum in 2005, the same year he graduated with a degree in Animal Biology from the University of Alberta. He continues to educate the public on all matters of the bug variety at the museum, caring for a host of species and giving presentations on natural history topics. Since 2006, Peter has been a guest on CBC Radio One's *Radioactive*, discussing anything and everything to do with insects as his alter ego, the "Bug Guy."

About the Illustrator

Peter Tyler

Peter Tyler is a graduate of the Vancouver Film School's Visual Art & Design, and Classical Animation programs. Though his ultimate passion is in filmmaking, he is also intent on developing his draftsmanship and storytelling, with the aim of using those skills in future filmic misadventures.

More trivia from Blue Bike Books...

GROSS AND DISGUSTING THINGS ABOUT THE HUMAN BODY

by Joanna Emery

The human body may be a wonder of natural engineering but it also can be pretty gross and bad-smelling. In this fearless little book, find the answers to such profound questions as why are boogers green, why do farts smell, and where does belly button lint come from?

$14.95 • ISBN: 978-1-897278-25-3 • 5.25" x 8.25" • 224 pages

WEIRD FOOD

by Joanna Emery

It's amazing what people will put in their mouths, and this book has most of them: frogs' legs, cow lips, salted scorpions, blood pudding, bird saliva, dirt, crocodile, insects... Keep an open mind—you might even find something you like!

$14.95 • ISBN: 978-1-897278-38-3 • 5.25" x 8.25" • 224 pages

Available from your local bookseller or by contacting the distributor,

Lone Pine Publishing

1-800-661-9017

www.lonepinepublishing.com